Turning Back the Fenians

New Brunswick's Last Colonial Campaign

D0658474

The New Brunswick Military Heritage Series, Volume 8

Turning Back the Fenians

NEW BRUNSWICK'S LAST COLONIAL CAMPAIGN

Robert L. Dallison

GOOSE LANE EDITIONS and
THE NEW BRUNSWICK MILITARY HERITAGE PROJECT

Edited by Brent Wilson.
Cover illustration detailed from PANB P5-712 showing New Brunswick Militia.
officers at the 1866 Camp of Instruction at Torryburn, NB.
Cover design by Lisa Rousseau.
Interior page design by Julie Scriver.
Printed in Canada.
10 9 8 7 6 5 4 3 2 1

Library and Archives Canada Cataloguing in Publication

Dallison, Robert L., 1935-
    Turning back the Fenians: New Brunswick's last colonial campaign / Robert L. Dallison.

(New Brunswick military heritage series; v.8)
Co-published with New Brunswick Military Heritage Project.
Includes bibliographical references and index.
ISBN 0-86492-461-5

1. New Brunswick — History — 1784-1867. 2. Canada — History — Fenian
Invasions, 1866-1870. I. New Brunswick Military Heritage Project
II. Title. III. Series.
FC2471.9.F4D34 2006   971.5'102   C2006-904336-1

Goose Lane Editions acknowledges the financial support of the Canada Council for the Arts, the Government of Canada through the Book Publishing Industry Development Program (BPIDP), and the New Brunswick Department of Wellness, Culture and Sport for its publishing activities.

Goose Lane Editions
Suite 330, 500 Beaverbrook Court
Fredericton, New Brunswick
CANADA E3B 5X4
www.gooselane.com

New Brunswick Military Heritage Project
The Brigadier Milton F. Gregg, VC,
Centre for the Study of War and Society
University of New Brunswick
PO Box 4400
Fredericton, New Brunswick
Canada   E3B 5A3
www.unb.ca/nbmhp

Contents

To Sharon, my wife and partner of half a century,
whose love, support, and encouragement make life worthwhile.

"HAVELOCK" VOLUNTEER RIFLE COMPANY,
ORGANIZATION—MARCH 14, 1860, PORTLAND, ST. JOHN, N. B.

No. 1 Company (Havelock Rifles) of the Saint John Volunteer Battalion, circa 1866-1867. The Havelock Rifles was one of the first volunteer militia companies formed in New Brunswick. NBM 1961-67

Introduction

New Brunswick's Indian Island lies uninhabited off the southeast corner of Deer Island, little noticed among the many beautiful islands in Passamaquoddy Bay. Today there is nothing to indicate that this small island was once an important trading depot on the border shared by New Brunswick and Maine and the scene of an international incident.

In 1866, Indian Island boasted a permanent resident population, a school, bonded warehouses and a customs house proudly flying the Union Jack, a flag that symbolized Great Britain and its worldwide empire. On Saturday, April 14, 1866, James Dixon, the customs officer on Indian Island, retired to bed after an exhausting and trying day caring for his ailing wife. Shortly after midnight, a violent knocking at the door and the ripping of shutters from their windows rudely awakened the Dixon family. Rushing to the door, Dixon was confronted by a body of armed men. Brandishing revolvers and threatening death to him and his family, they demanded Dixon hand over the British flag that flew over the customs house. Although he was reluctant to comply, the pleading of his frightened wife, who was concerned for the safety of their family, prompted Dixon to surrender his beloved Union Jack. Once back in Maine, the raiders jubilantly claimed a major victory. They triumphantly sent the flag to New York, where it was flaunted as a trophy of war. The American press made much of the fact that the British flag had been

Earliest known photograph of Indian Island dated prior to 1900. Campobello Island is in the background, left centre is Cherry Island, and Marble Island is to the right. The white house in the centre is the Moses residence. PANB P8-298.

"captured" under the supposedly watchful eye of the Royal Navy, proclaiming that the incident "will cause the British lion to shake his sides and lash his tail. Let him! The spirit of liberty is abroad."

The armed band that terrorized the Dixon family were members of the Fenian Brotherhood, a revolutionary movement organized in Ireland with the goal of establishing an independent Irish Republic by armed force. It found support among the many Irish immigrants in the United States. To assist their Irish brothers in freeing Ireland, the Fenians conceived of a plan to invade British North America, with the goal of holding it hostage. With its large Irish population and undefended borders, New Brunswick appeared to be an ideal target, and a group of Fenians plotted to seize Campobello Island.

When the Fenians gathered along the Maine border in the spring of 1866, the people of New Brunswick felt vulnerable and feared for their safety. Mysterious and inexplicable Fenian activities, incursions, alarms and alerts increased the tension. Thanks to the leadership displayed by an energetic lieutenant-governor, effective defensive measures were eventually taken by the New Brunswick militia. Support from Great Britain followed, with British soldiers and a squadron of warships dispatched to the Bay of Fundy. By May 1866, the Fenians in Maine, recognizing that

New Brunswick was no longer an easy target, dispersed and turned their focus on central Canada.

Although the Fenian crisis is now largely forgotten, it has left an enduring legacy, both militarily and politically. As the crisis unfolded, a number of concurrent themes emerged. First, in 1860, the New Brunswick militia was disorganized and in no state to contribute to the defence of the province. The initial task facing the commander-in-chief was to develop an effective local militia. By the end of the Fenian affair, local military forces had turned out in large numbers and helped to turn back this threat. Second, with the outbreak of the American Civil War, the relationship between the province of New Brunswick and its neighbours in the United States had rapidly deteriorated. With the arrival of the Fenians along the frontier, the reaction of the people of Maine would be decisive in shaping the outcome of the crisis. Third, with a large proportion of New Brunswick's population being Irish or of Irish descent, provincial authorities were concerned over their response to the Fenian cause. Would it reignite the bitter sectarian conflict between Catholic and Protestant that had plagued the province in the 1840s? Finally, a backdrop to the Fenian crisis was the ongoing struggle for the confederation of the provinces of British North America. The Fenian attacks came at a time when the confederation debate in New Brunswick had intensified to red-hot levels, and it tipped the balance in favour of Confederation.

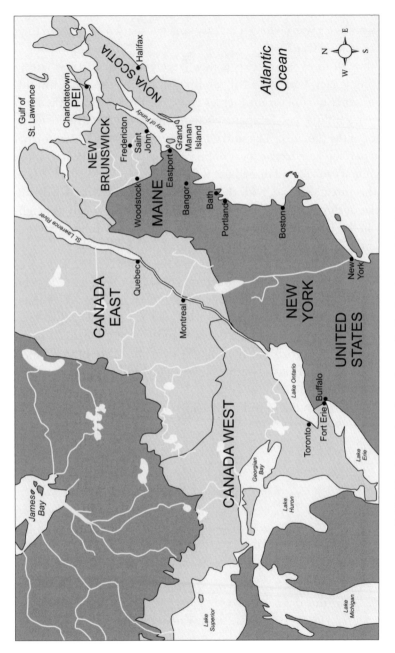

British North America, the region under Fenian threat, 1865-1866. Mike Bechthold

Chapter One

The Fenian Brotherhood

The band of marauders that landed on Indian Island in the dead of night to terrorize the provincial customs officer and his family were members of the Fenian Brotherhood, intent on freeing Ireland from Great Britain. The British flag flying over the customs house was clearly visible from Eastport, Maine, and stood for everything the Brotherhood abhorred. Although the incident at the Dixon home had the appearance of comic opera, to the Fenians it was a blow for justice and liberty against an uncompromising tyrant.

The Fenian Brotherhood was one of many revolutionary groups found on the long and difficult road to Irish independence. The idea of an independent Ireland which was rooted in the Potato Famine, had had a profound effect on the people of Ireland and was instrumental in inspiring revolutionary nationalism. An ill-conceived insurrection in 1848 by a group called Young Ireland was quickly crushed by British authorities. James Stephen, a member of the defeated Young Ireland movement, fled to Paris, where he dedicated himself to enhancing his conspiratorial skills. A decade later, Stephen was back in Dublin organizing a secret revolutionary society called the Irish Republican Brotherhood, better known as the Fenians. Under Stephen's leadership, the movement spread rapidly throughout Ireland amongst labourers, shopkeepers, and others hit hard by the depression of the early 1860s.

John O'Mahony, another member of the Young Ireland movement, fled to New York. In concert with Stephen, O'Mahony began organizing Irish immigrants in the United States to support Stephen's proposed insurrection with money, munitions and volunteers. O'Mahony named his group the Fenian Brotherhood, after a legendary band of Irish warriors called *Fianna*.

Irish immigrants flooded into the United States during and after the Potato Famine. By 1860, there were more Irish citizens living in New York City than in any city in Ireland; more than a quarter of the city's population of 800,000 was Irish-born. Most of these immigrants were fiercely patriotic to Ireland and had bitter memories of perceived injustices inflicted by Britain. The Fenian leadership appealed to the American Irish by using familiar slogans, such as "for liberty" and "free speech." The Fenian Brotherhood grew quickly, and by 1863 its leaders claimed 10,000 enrolled members in America. Drilling became a popular social activity, the participants motivated by the goal of Irish emancipation. A quarter of a million dollars and large quantities of war material were readily raised to support Fenian activities.

The end of the American Civil War presented the Fenian Brotherhood with a golden opportunity. In May 1865, there had been more than one million soldiers in the Union Army, and six months later, eighty percent of the army had been disbanded, leaving many unemployed, battle-hardened soldiers seeking new pursuits. Thousands of them were Irish by birth or descent; thus the pool of restless veterans provided a ready source of fighting men for the Fenian cause. Recruiting agents spoke of military glory, the eternal gratitude of the Irish and a promise of a substantial bounty upon enrolling. The front pages of major American newspapers provided glowing and, for the most part, grossly exaggerated accounts of the Fenian organization, its leaders, their objectives and activities. The anti-British bias displayed in most of these newspapers found general approval with the American public, both because of the long-standing hostility towards Britain and because Britain had been sympathetic to the Confederacy during the Civil War. Taking advantage of this popularity, particularly in areas with large Irish populations, local politicians voiced support for the Fenian cause. The Fenian leadership exploited both the media attention and its political power.

The growth of the Fenian movement in both Ireland and America did not go unnoticed by British authorities. An insurrection appeared imminent in Ireland. Membership in the Brotherhood was reported as several hundred thousand, and rumours abounded concerning large sums of money arriving from the United States to support its activities. Tension increased when an American sailing ship called *Erin's Hope,* loaded with rifles, ammunition, assorted war materials and a party of volunteers, was intercepted off a secluded Irish cove by the Royal Navy. On September 14, 1865, working on information provided by a double agent, the British authorities took decisive action. The Brotherhood's newspaper, the *Irish People,* was raided, its staff arrested and further publication suppressed. Incriminating documents seized in the raid identified the Brotherhood's leadership, which led to further arrests and the dismantling of the secret organization. James Stephen was taken into custody, but he soon managed to escape, fleeing first to France and then to the United States. The insurrection was crushed before it began, and the Brotherhood in Ireland ceased to exist. The winning of Ireland's freedom now rested squarely on the American wing of the Fenian Brotherhood.

The Fenian Brotherhood held its third national convention in October 1865 in Philadelphia, Pennsylvania. With the dramatic events in Ireland as a backdrop, more than six hundred delegates gathered from all over North America. After a stirring address by the fugitive James Stephen, the assembly set about tackling the crisis facing the Fenian movement. John O'Mahony's leadership was challenged as too cautious by a group of militants calling themselves "men of action." They were particularly critical of O'Mahony's apparent reluctance to commence hostilities against Britain. The militants orchestrated major changes to the Brotherhood's organization and constitution. O'Mahony was forced to accept an elected presidency and was shorn of much of his power, and found himself immediately in conflict with William Randall Roberts, the president of a newly created senate. The constitutional changes made Roberts the rallying point for the anti-O'Mahony faction.

Given the existing circumstances, the "men of action" under Roberts believed that an insurrection in Ireland was unlikely to succeed and a more effective course of action would be to invade and seize British North America. They argued that the Province of Canada, the area now known as Ontario and Quebec, could be captured with ease, and, once Canada was occupied, the Canadians could be easily convinced of the justice of the Fenian cause. Then, using Canada as a base, attacks could be launched against Britain and its seaborne commerce. If this scheme was not totally successful, the Fenians hoped they could create sufficient friction to spark a conflict between the United States and Great Britain. An Anglo-American war could only benefit the cause of Ireland's independence. At the Philadelphia convention, Brigadier General Thomas Sweeny, a distinguished veteran of the Union Army, was elected secretary of war and appointed commander-in-chief. He was charged by the Roberts faction with developing an invasion plan for the province of Canada.

The Philadelphia convention ended with a fundamental split within the Fenian Brotherhood. The "men of action" under Roberts planned to raise a large army and invade Canada, while those under O'Mahony's leadership clung to the original concept of sponsoring an insurrection within Ireland. In late 1865, to raise money to support the uprising in Ireland, O'Mahony issued bonds, calling the series "Bonds of the Irish Republic." He was accused of violating the Brotherhood's constitution and the Roberts faction attempted to depose him, but he retaliated by expelling them from the Fenian headquarters. The break was complete and final, and the Fenian Brotherhood was torn into two bitterly hostile factions.

On January 2, 1866, O'Mahony called a meeting of the Fenian Brotherhood in New York City. His supporters packed the convention, reinstated the pre-Philadelphia constitution and reaffirmed the goal of supporting insurrection in Ireland. The Roberts faction responded by holding a meeting in Pittsburgh in February 1866. There, they unveiled and approved General "Fighting Tom" Sweeny's master plan for the invasion of Canada. Sweeny immediately began to gather a staff and prepare for a spring campaign.

British authorities carefully watched these developments and took the threat from both factions seriously. On February 19, 1866, a special session of the British parliament suspended the right to *habeas corpus* in Ireland. By this curtailment of basic civil rights, parliament hoped to avoid further domestic unrest and violence. More arrests in Ireland followed, including 150 Irish Americans. The reaction in America was immediate. The tales of Americans languishing in British prisons facing an uncertain fate galvanized both factions of the Fenian Brotherhood into action. They held mass rallies throughout the United States. O'Mahony, addressing a large rally in New York City, called the British "the foul tyrants of our race" and pleaded for more money "to put munitions of war in the hands of the Irish army . . . [and] to put Irish ships upon the sea."

The strong reaction to the British suspension of *habeas corpus* in Ireland had a direct impact on the O'Mahony faction of the Fenian Brotherhood. In order to maintain its leadership role, the Brotherhood could no longer be content with fomenting rebellion in Ireland; it needed to take some form of overt action against Britain. The secretary of the treasury, Bernard Doran Killian, as part of a Fenian delegation, asked both President Andrew Jackson and Secretary of State William H. Seward what position the United States would take if the Fenians seized British territory north of the American border in support of an insurrection in Ireland. The response from both was sufficiently vague to encourage Killian to formulate a plan of attack. On St. Patrick's Day in 1866, he proposed capturing Campobello Island in New Brunswick, an isolated island in the western approaches of Passamaquoddy Bay within easy reach of Maine. The Fenians would use the island as a base for privateering attacks on British shipping in the North Atlantic, for organizing an invasion of Ireland, and for conducting offensive operations against British interests. There was reason to believe that New Brunswick, with its substantial Irish population, would welcome Fenian intervention and the opportunity to shed British domination.

Although not as ambitious as the invasion of Canada proposed by the Roberts and Sweeny faction, Killian argued, a military success

EASTPORT ME., April 10, 1866.

The President of the Covnention hereby thanks the Delegates for their promptness and discipline, and trust that, whilst waiting instructions from the Central Office, the Delegates will make due allowance for the civic inconveniences. All has been done that could be done to consult their comfort, and the President need only, in further sustainment of his zeal, allude to the very many downright hardships and sufferings nesessarily undergone by our soldiers in the late war,—sufferings and privations lengthened and intensified owing to English Neutrality. He has no doubt, however, that the same spirit which animated our soldiers will inspire our civilians; and that the deliberations of their Convention will be marked by wisdom and decorum.—

On receipt of necessary intelligence, the President will proceed to develope the subject matters to be discussed by the Convention. For the time being the Delegates will fraternize with the good people of Eastport, and have opportunities of appreciating its many natural advantages, as the Frontier City of the representative Republic.

B. DORAN KILLIAN,

Pres't of Convention.

Fenian handbill issued by Bernard Doran Killian at Eastport, Maine, on 10 April 1866. PANB RS558D was absolutely necessary; only "by striking a blow and making a fight" could the Brotherhood's reputation be sustained. A deciding factor was Killian's assertion that the United States would take a neutral stance and not interfere with the Brotherhood's activities along the Maine border. Against his better judgment, O'Mahony reluctantly approved Killian's plan. Without delay, they collected funds, gathered arms, recruited men and purchased a steamer. The New York *Herald* excitedly reported on April 5, 1866, that a Fenian expedition consisting of three steamboats with three thousand experienced soldiers had sailed to capture Bermuda. The next day the *Herald* reported that a second expedition had sailed under Killian's command, consisting of two steamships with twenty-five hundred men onboard. At the time, no one realized that these reports were wildly exaggerated.

Arthur Hamilton Gordon, first Lord Stanmore, the
lieutenant-governor of New Brunswick during the
Fenian crisis. PANB P515-84.

Chapter Two

Double Agents, Loose Lips
and Rampant Rumour

In early 1866, with the collapse of the revolutionary movement in Ireland, the struggle for Irish independence devolved on the Fenian Brotherhood in North America. In order to retain a position of leadership and maintain its essential public support, the Brotherhood had to take direct overt action in support of its goal against Great Britain. Both rival factions of the Fenian Brotherhood opted to attack British North America: the group led by Roberts was determined to invade the Province of Canada, and the O'Mahony party elected to seize Campobello Island in New Brunswick. Before developing their counter measures, authorities in both Britain and British North America sought reliable intelligence on Fenian plans and capabilities, which required them to separate fact from the many fanciful newspaper and public reports. They also had to determine what support the Fenian Brotherhood could expect from within New Brunswick and Maine. Strong public reaction to the perceived threat posed by the Fenians forced the New Brunswick government to finally act.

Maintaining security and the secrecy of their plans were not the Fenian Brotherhood's strong points. Public discussion, heated debates in open conventions and bombastic bragging generated considerable public interest and attracted extensive newspaper coverage. Beginning as early as the fall of 1864, sensational news concerning the Fenian movement spread throughout British North America, particularly in the Province of Canada. George Brown, politician and owner of the *Toronto Globe*, strongly believed that the Fenians would shortly embark on a wave of violence and announced in an editorial that "It is certain we have in our midst an armed, secret organization." The powerful Orange Order went further, claiming that all Roman Catholics and everyone of Irish descent were either Fenians or potential Fenians. Credence was provided when delegates from Montreal, Quebec City, Toronto and Hamilton attended the Fenian convention in Chicago. Tension in Toronto increased when a group called the Hibernian Benevolent Society was formed under the leadership of Michael Murphy, with a reported strength of six hundred members. The Society's stated purpose was to protect Catholics from Orangemen, but it received Fenian support and its real purpose was in question. Conflict seemed inevitable when the Roberts faction of the Brotherhood advocated an armed invasion of Canada and General Sweeny formally presented his plan of attack. Thomas D'Arcy McGee, the popular politician from Montreal, attempted to ease the tension and separate Fenians from the majority of Irish Canadians. As a teenager, McGee had been part of the unsuccessful Young Ireland movement. Later in life, he became an influential politician and owned a Montreal newspaper called *New Era,* in which he advocated a "new nationality" for British North America that would provide justice and freedom for all. He loudly denounced the Fenians as "a seditious Irish society" and referred to the movement as a "foreign disease" and "political leprosy."

More balanced and factual reports about the Fenian's activities were routinely prepared by British diplomatic and consular officials in the United States. They monitored events and were alert to changes within the Fenian movement. They were assisted by a multitude of spies and informers, some paid and some not, who permeated the Fenian organization. British-paid informers included such high profile Fenians as "Red" Jim McDermott, a close confidant of O'Mahony, and Rudolph Fitzpatrick, the Brotherhood's assistant secretary. As a result, British officials were aware of the most intimate details of Fenian decisions and activities. They knew, for example, that the Fenian leadership had influential friends at the highest level of the United States government and that they were lobbying for covert American support by stressing the debt owed the Irish people for their major contribution to the Union during the Civil War. Sir Frederick Bruce, the British ambassador in Washington, attempted to meet with American government officials to discuss the Fenian Brotherhood and their anti-British activities. He had little success because he could not get government officials to agree that Fenian activities were either illegal or inappropriate. Secretary of State Seward, who was well known for his pro-Irish sympathies, informed Bruce that reports of Fenian activities were exaggerated and unworthy of discussion. In mid-November 1865, Bruce formally protested to the American government about "the Fenian agitators in the United States." With an upcoming congressional election, American politicians found themselves in the uncomfortable position of needing the Irish American vote, even at the expense of British goodwill.

In mid-September 1865, Edward Archibald, the British consul general in New York City, sent an urgent message to Governor General Charles Stanley Monck in Ottawa warning of possible Fenian incursions. John A. Macdonald, the minister of militia, had at his disposal a small "detective force" to monitor Fenian activities south of the border, and, in response to this warning, both the force and the budget were increased. The Canadian government was sufficiently concerned that on November 9, 1865, it called out nine companies of volunteer militia for several months to protect vital points along the frontier. At the same time, based on reports from Washington, the colonial secretary, Edward Cardwell, warned the lieutenant-governor of New Brunswick, Arthur Hamilton Gordon, of possible Fenian attacks across the Maine border. The editor of St. Stephen's *St. Croix Courier,* noting the threat of a Fenian invasion to Canada, concluded that New Brunswick faced an identical risk. He urged defensive measures be taken immediately to secure the border. Unlike the Canadian government, the government of New Brunswick opted to bide its time.

It is difficult to gauge how much support the Fenian Brotherhood had in New Brunswick. On November 3, 1865, the Saint John *Morning News* reported that a delegate from the city had attended a Fenian convention and "a Fenian organization, no doubts, exists in this Province."

The article suggested that an "organized invasion" was unlikely, but that some form of a raid could be expected during the winter, and that "banks may be robbed, and other injuries inflicted." It went on to complain that it was "unaccountable that no measures had been taken to avert such dangers." An editorial in the *Carleton Sentinel* of Woodstock stated, "We believe that in the Province there are Fenians, or at all events, what is equally bad, Fenian sympathizers, and therefore believe it to be the duty of our Government to take the necessary steps" to protect the province. The *Burning Bush*, an Orange Order newspaper, warned its readers that twelve-thousand Fenians were prepared to rise on a moment's notice. The threat renewed anti-Catholic feeling in the province and strengthened the Orange Order. In a speech in Woodstock, Lieutenant-Governor Gordon acknowledged the threat posed by the Fenians, but he said he was more concerned with the threat from within. He feared that the Fenian crisis could divide New Brunswickers "into two hostile camps, viewing each other with suspicion or hatred," a circumstance that would take a very long time to heal. He was troubled by those who linked Fenianism with Catholicism. He found ridiculous the idea that, since some Fenians were Catholics, all Catholics were Fenians. He was quick to point out that many Fenians were Protestants and many more professed to no religion whatsoever. As Gordon travelled the province, this became his constant theme, and he emphasized the loyalty displayed by Roman Catholics in the past. Gordon received support from members of the clergy. Father E. J. Dunphy of St. Stephen branded Fenianism a delusion and strongly denounced revolution in all its forms. He urged his parishioners to be worthy of Gordon's confidence in them. On St. Patrick's Day in 1866, Archbishop Thomas Connolly of Halifax, whose jurisdiction included New Brunswick, made a public address denouncing Fenianism in the strongest of terms:

> Their scheme as now appears to me, is simply this, let us under the green flag of Erin, invade the territory of our unoffending neighbors. In the name of liberty and eman-

cipation of Ireland, with the scum of disbanded soldiers of the north, let us invade the British Provinces, and rob their homesteads, and trample down their liberties . . . let us cut the throats of four million, if needed, of a people against whom we have no cause of offence.

He followed this address with a letter to the Saint John *Globe* urging Catholics not to encourage Fenian violence. Connolly argued that the Roman Catholic Irish of British North America possessed a social and political freedom that they could find nowhere else and that the United States had nothing better to offer. The effect of these appeals is difficult to assess, but during the crisis that followed, the Fenian Brotherhood found little support in New Brunswick.

The Fenians had also hoped to take advantage of the strained relations that had developed between New Brunswick and Maine during the American Civil War. The situation had deteriorated as a result of the pro-Confederate sympathy displayed within New Brunswick, the *Trent* affair, which had brought Britain and the United States to the brink of war, and the disruption of routine trade. Americans were also incensed by the *Chesapeake* affair, during which an enterprising self-proclaimed Southerner and a gang of "Confederates," composed almost entirely of New Brunswickers, captured an American steamer, then escaped justice, thanks to the intervention of Maritimers. Then, in 1864, four Confederate soldiers under the command of Captain William Collins crossed the St. Croix River at St. Stephen and attempted to rob a Calais bank. The raiders walked into a trap and were promptly captured. After being sent to the state prison for attempted armed robbery, Collins escaped and, to the great annoyance of Maine authorities, found sanctuary in New Brunswick. The people of Maine were exasperated with their neighbours, and the *Calais Advertiser* complained bitterly about pro-Southern sympathies across the border. When the Fenians posed a threat to New Brunswick, this bitterness still lingered, and the *Eastport Sentinel* recounted the days during the Civil War when the province harboured pirates and robbers. The *Machias Republican* went further, stating "The

Provincials are terribly frightened, which is pleasant for us to contemplate. They are now reaping what they sowed a little time ago."

Despite these feelings, the Fenians found little support in Maine. The majority of Mainers were curious onlookers and chose to maintain an attitude of friendly neutrality; a neutrality that was monitored by British consuls in Portland, Bath, Eastport and Bangor. During his visit to the frontier, Lieutenant-Governor Gordon was pleased to find a cooperative spirit prevailing across the border. The mayor of Calais received a unanimous vote of thanks from the St. Stephen magistrates when he assured the governor that he would keep his neighbours across the border informed of any Fenian activities in his community. In early December 1865, a British secret agent toured Maine and reported that he found no evidence of dangerous Fenian activity in Portland, Lewiston, Eastport, Calais or Bangor.

Nevertheless, disturbing news from further south continued and panic gripped the port city of Saint John on Wednesday, December 6, 1865. The newspapers in both the United States and New Brunswick had been following events within the Fenian Brotherhood for months. The coverage, a sensational and confusing mixture of fact, opinion and exaggeration, intensified when Sweeny's plan to invade Canada and Killian's proposal to seize Campobello Island were unveiled. Accounts provided by supposed eye-witnesses and self-proclaimed experts added to the excitement. The lieutenant-governor had obtained considerable intelligence on the Fenians, but it was not until he received an encoded message from Sir Frederick Bruce in Washington on Tuesday, December 5, that he decided the time had come to act. Not wishing to increase public unease, he opted to visit the frontier communities and brief their leaders personally on the situation. Before leaving Fredericton, he sent a telegram to the Honourable Albert James Smith, leader of the New Brunswick government, who was at home in Dorchester preparing for the Christmas holidays, requesting Smith join him immediately in St. Stephen. Word circulated rapidly that Gordon had received a ciphered message from Washington.

Speculation quickly spread that a Fenian attack on New Brunswick

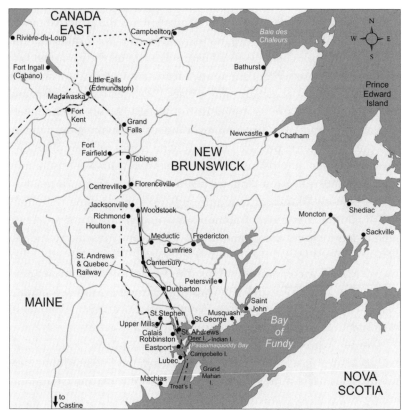

The New Brunswick and Maine Border Region, 1865-1866. Mike Bechthold

was imminent, a view enhanced by Gordon's sudden and unannounced trip to the frontier. The urgency of the situation was further heightened when Smith was seen hurriedly passing through Saint John during the night, having been unceremoniously summoned from the comforts of his home in inclement weather. Saint John officials immediately concluded that if the frontier communities were under threat so was the City of Saint John, which was vulnerable to all forms of seaborne attack. Not burdened by modesty, city officials decided that there was little of value to plunder in the frontier communities and that any discriminating Fenian freebooter would select Saint John as the preferred target. Its many banks would prove particularly lucrative, the local banks and military authorities both agreed. There was a run on the banks, and officials took steps to secure their assets. Lieutenant Colonel Grierson, the garrison commander at Saint John, placed his men on high alert and telegraphed Halifax requesting a British warship be sent immediately to protect the harbour. They mounted cannons overlooking the harbour, and the local militia prepared to guard vital points and patrol around the city. Lieutenant Colonels John Thurgar and John Robertson, militia commanders in Saint John, telegraphed Gordon asking, "Is the danger sufficiently imminent to require officers commanding Battalions to call out the militia under Section forty-nine militia act. If so, please send orders for arms and ammunition." The recently installed telegraph network helped spread the panic to Fredericton, Woodstock, and other New Brunswick communities. Even the *Boston Pilot* reported the excitement in Saint John under the heading "Expected Fenian Raid into New Brunswick." Anticipating a Fenian raid, the *Carleton Sentinel* in Woodstock advised its readers to "keep the powder dry."

Gordon's attempt to restrain public reaction to a potential Fenian raid had failed miserably. Thanks to the excitement in Saint John, New Brunswickers across the province were thoroughly alarmed. Gordon's annoyance is clear in a letter he sent to the mayor of Saint John dated December 7, 1865: "I am sorry to perceive from the newspapers that general alarm appears to prevail at St. John in consequence of its being imagined there that I have received intelligence . . . of the intention on the part of the so-called Fenian Association to invade the Province and attack St. John. I have received no such information, and I do not believe that any ground exists for such an apprehension." He went on to explain how unlikely he thought such an attack was. In summary, he said had there been the slightest reason to believe that Saint John was threatened, "that it is to Saint John and not to the frontier that I should have at once repaired. I trust that you will take every means in your power to abate the excitement, which has been, in my opinion, too needlessly created."

Despite Gordon's assurances to the contrary, there was now no doubt in the public's mind that the Fenian Brotherhood posed an imminent threat to the peace and security of New Brunswick. The government could no longer delay taking protective measures. The responsibility for the defence of the province lay squarely with Lieutenant-Governor Gordon, the commander-in-chief.

Lieutenant-Governor Gordon and his staff on the steps of Old Government House, Fredericton. PANB P5-897

Chapter Three

The Volunteer Militia

By the beginning of 1866, the growth of the Fenian Brotherhood and their increased activities had created considerable unease in New Brunswick. The public felt very vulnerable, and newspapers demanded that the government take immediate action to protect the province. These concerns turned the focus onto the provincial militia.

In 1787, the New Brunswick legislature had passed a militia act requiring that every man between the ages of sixteen and sixty be enrolled in the militia. Those who failed to appear, properly equipped, at the annual muster parade were fined. This system successfully met the military crises that confronted the province in the early years, but by the 1850s the militia had become ineffective and was in need of major reform. Moreover, the British government felt that it had carried total responsibility for imperial defence long enough – the long-suffering British taxpayer deserved relief. With the advent of responsible government in the provinces of British North America, British authorities felt strongly that part of the burden for defence should be passed to the provinces and the British garrisons reduced, if not eliminated completely. The New Brunswick government, however, had absolutely no desire to assume any responsibility for defence. In 1852, the legislative assembly obstinately suspended the militia act and all defence expenditures. It argued that relations with the United States had been excellent since the settlement of the Maine border dispute and New Brunswick faced no possibility of a war of its own making; therefore, the province had no need for expensive defence measures. Stoutly resisting pressure from the British Colonial Office, members of the legislature held firm to their belief that colonial defence was an imperial and not a provincial matter.

This impasse dissolved with the reappearance of cross-border tension and the spread of a volunteer militia movement. During the Napoleonic Wars, military units formed voluntarily across Britain to defend the country against a French invasion. In 1859, when Napoleon III again threatened to invade England, the volunteer response was overwhelming and the British militia was revitalized. Major General Sir William Fenwick Williams, the general officer commanding the British regular forces in Canada, suggested that this volunteer movement could be successfully and beneficially transported to North America. The concept quickly gained acceptance, and, with Williams's assistance, volunteer militia companies sprang up across New Brunswick. The legislature could not resist this patriotic groundswell and was forced to provide the necessary legislation and funds to support it. By March 1860, thirteen voluntary infantry companies and six voluntary artillery batteries had been created. The first public appearance of the volunteer militia occurred during the visit of the Prince of Wales in 1860. Its impressive appearance and performance during this visit resulted in wide public acclaim for the volunteer movement in New Brunswick.

The Honourable Arthur Hamilton Gordon assumed his post as lieutenant-governor of New Brunswick in mid-October 1861. His aristocratic background and temperament did not prepare him for the rough and tumble responsible government practised in colonial New Brunswick. Although his powers were limited, they did exist, and he was fiercely protective of them. In addition to being lieutenant-governor, Gordon was also commander-in-chief of the New Brunswick militia, one area where he could discharge his duties without political interference.

Facing growing tension with the northern states involved in the American Civil War, New Brunswick politicians were soon forced to recognize the need for an effective defence force. In 1861, the *Trent* Affair brought Britain and the United States to the brink of war. When the USS *Jacinto* stopped the British Royal Mail Packet *Trent* upon the high seas and forcibly removed two Confederate agents, the British public was inflamed and demanded action. In response, Britain sent eleven thousand British regular soldiers to reinforce the North American garrisons. Late in December 1861, with little warning, ships arrived in Saint John with 6,823 British regulars who were to be transported over several hundred miles of snow-covered wilderness to the St. Lawrence River Valley. Saint John lacked the necessary facilities to handle an influx of that size, and the road and rail systems were totally inadequate. Although not strictly within his area of responsibility, Gordon assumed control of the support activities within New Brunswick. He commandeered schools, temperance halls, customs houses and any place else that could provide accommodation. He made arrangement for beds, bedding, stoves and other supplies. He called on the local militia to do sentry duty, construct and staff overnight halting places, and police the route to prevent desertion by passing British soldiers. Thanks to brilliant military staff work and the excellent support provided by Gordon, the move of the British reinforcements in midwinter occurred smoothly and without a single fatality. The appearance of this large number of soldiers in a time of crisis greatly boosted New Brunswickers' morale, as it demonstrated that in time of need Britain was committed to the protection of her colonies. However, this event added not a single soldier or cannon to the defence of the province.

Following the *Trent* Affair, Gordon set up a commission of selected officers to review the state of the militia and make recommendations. The result was the innovative *Militia Act* of 1862 and a vote of two thousand pounds annually for three years put into effect the recommendations. The new act divided the active militia into three components. Class A consisted of able-bodied men of military age who volunteered to undergo military training. This group was formed into cavalry, artillery, engineer and infantry units. Classes B and C consisted of all other male inhabitants of the province between the ages of sixteen and forty-five, with Class B being unmarried men and widowers without children, and Class C being married men and widowers with children. These two classes were required to assemble one day annually for enrolment and training. All men between the ages of forty-five and sixty belonged to the sedentary militia.

Taking advantage of his experience with the volunteer movement in his native Scotland and using the full authority of his office as commander-in-chief, Gordon set about improving the effectiveness of the New Brunswick militia. He was ably assisted in this task by a series of efficient adjutants general, all of whom were professional British army officers. Gordon and his staff maintained tight control over promotions and the granting of commissions, brooking no political interference. All new commissions were limited to a five-year period, and officers were required to pass a drill examination before taking up an appointment. Those over the age of sixty or physically unfit were retired. Volunteer companies were to number not less than forty men and no more than seventy-five. Those units that fell below minimum strength were disbanded. Arms and accoutrements were issued to volunteer companies, but to ensure security and proper maintenance, they were kept in public armories. Funds were provided for the rental of drill halls and rifle competitions. In addition to the training conducted by their own officers, the militia received six days of training annually under an experienced paid drill instructor. Eight experienced drill instructors arrived from the British Army to perform this function. To assess the effectiveness of his reforms and directives, Gordon visited and inspected the militia units regularly and frequently.

Gordon was personally involved in all aspects of the provincial militia and did not hesitate to enforce the *Militia Act*. The 1863 Order No. 2 declared, "His Excellency the Commander-in-Chief learns with regret from the Monthly Progress Returns, that the members of several of the Volunteer Companies of militia are extremely remiss in their attendance at drill." Gordon warned that if there was no improvement he would disband ineffective companies. True to his word, he disbanded several units. In September 1864, the commander-in-chief dispensed with the service of the Richibucto Company of Volunteers, which had "fallen below the strength by Law." In March 1865, the artillery battery commanded by Captain M'Lachlan, having "for a long time been irregular and unsatisfactory," was disbanded. "In consequence of the Report of a Court of Enquiry . . . his Excellency has been pleased to dispense with the services of Captain Sandford, and the Officers and Men composing the Volunteer Company under his command" from the 1st Battalion Charlotte County Militia. Nothing escaped Gordon's notice: "The Commander-in-Chief desires to impress upon Officers commanding Companies, that the custom of permitting their men to keep their own arms and accoutrements, is directly in opposition to Section 13 of the Militia Act." He pointed out that commanding officers were given forty dollars to defray the cost of weapon storage. Gordon also used the Militia General Orders for public commendations. For example, in September 1863, Lieutenant Colonel Stephen K. Foster of the New Brunswick Regiment of Artillery and Lieutenant Colonel Honourable John Robertson were congratulated on the good performance of their units at a military review at Camp Torryburn, outside Saint John, which had been the first opportunity that they had had to work with British regulars.

Despite these charges, Gordon and his military staff faced many obstacles. It proved difficult to maintain volunteer units in rural areas because of the demands imposed by frequent drill parades and the distance volunteers had to travel. As a result, volunteer units were concentrated in urban centres, with half of the companies located in Saint John. It was also difficult to expand the number of volunteer units because the available pool of recruits was restricted. The average labourer worked at least twelve hours a day, six days a week, leaving little time for military training. It was hard to find men of ability and proven leadership willing to make the necessary commitment to accept positions of command. In addition, there was the usual spate of local jealousies and complaints with which to contend. The petty complaint that some volunteer units had been favoured with the prized short Enfield rifle annoyed Gordon. With some irritation, he explained that only long Enfield rifles had been issued in New Brunswick, although "It is obviously impossible that all

Companies should be armed with Rifles of exactly the same date and some Rifles have shorter stocks than others."

Class A volunteer units were the main priority, and they received most of the available resources and funds. The other two classes continued to exist, but their effectiveness varied widely. In October 1865, the Fredericton *Headquarters* reported on the annual muster of the local companies. "The muster was merely for the purpose of calling the roll and ascertaining numbers. Some of the companies mustered in good force, others hardly quarter strength. Some of the officers appeared *en regle* in uniform, others without any badge of any rank. The whole affair went off very quiet and orderly." A letter to the editor signed by "Flat Foot" commenting on the same muster provided a very different picture:

> Sir, how can I describe the gathering assembled. Between ten and eleven o'clock, the Colonel and Adjutant (in uniform) might be seen on horseback riding here and there, and the Sergeant Major, with an armful of books, rushing in different directions, endeavoring to post his Sergeants, as I afterwards judged. Here might be seen one or two officers in full (undress) uniforms; there another batch with a sword alone; others with a pencil or roll call to distinguish them from privates. Then, as to men, what can I say, as it would be impossible to do justice to them in a description of the scene. One company mustered perhaps 75 men, and the rest of the companies ranged from that down to about 20 each; and those composed principally of over aged men and boys.

Flat Foot called it "a farce" and claimed he attended only to avoid the fine.

For the same muster period, the Saint John *Morning News* reported that "veterans to Col. Robertson's Battalion of the City Light Infantry were called upon to assemble themselves on the Barrack Square to answer the roll-call and perform certain other military formalities . . . Promotions among the officers during the past year seems to have been so great and transfers so extensive, that mostly all the Companies have got new Captains. This, together with the rain, caused a good deal of confusion among the 'Rank and File,' who kept wandering about in all directions searching eagerly for their missing chief." A very critical description of the muster followed. Three days later, the same newspaper made a more complimentary report on the muster of the Saint John City Rifles. Nine companies were on a parade, with five or six hundred men in attendance, all officers except one were in uniform, and all companies "were put through sundry movements." It said that "Lieutenant Colonel Thurgar, who was in command of the force, did himself ample justice." Similarly, William C. Anslow noted in his diary that on a beautiful September day in 1865 he went up the Miramichi River about a mile above Wilson's Point to attend the annual militia muster. "There were a large number present and after some time had elapsed, were formed into line & the names called. They were then marched up & formed into a kind of square & were then addressed by the Governor & then dismissed." It had been intended that the annual muster include drill instruction. However, this proved unworkable due to the lack of qualified instructors and the untrained men proved both awkward and unruly. The drill training during the annual muster was abandoned for a simple assembling and roll call. The result was that the bulk of the Class B and C militia was a mere paper force. To face the Fenian crisis, it was clear that the defence of New Brunswick would rest on the Class A volunteer militia and British regulars.

Gordon appointed a second militia commission to review the success of the *Militia Act* of 1862 and make further recommendations. The result was the *Militia Act* of 1865, which provided that grants to volunteer companies would be based proportionately on their strength and this strength would include only men who had attended at least fifteen drills in a six-month period. A major innovation called for the establishment of annual camps of instruction, of twenty-eight days duration, designed to train volunteers who would in turn train their home units. The first camp of instruction was held in Fredericton in July 1865, with 947 volunteers quartered in the Exhibition Hall. They were treated like profes-

Training battalion on parade during the Camp of Instruction at the Fredericton Exhibition Grounds, July 1865. PANB P5-378

sionals, governed by the Code of Military Discipline, drilled by qualified drill instructors and paid a small allowance. The camp commandant was Captain H. J. Hallowes, an experienced regular British officer, and the instructors were provided by the 15th Regiment from the Fredericton British garrison. It was an unqualified success and provided another boost to the volunteer movement in New Brunswick. By 1866, as a result of Gordon's determination and energy, the force consisted of 2,099 volunteers organized into seven troops of cavalry, ten batteries of artillery, one company of engineers and twenty-one companies of infantry. As small and inadequate as this volunteer militia was, New Brunswick could be thankful that Gordon's reforms had occurred prior to the arrival of the Fenian Brotherhood on the Maine border.

Chapter Four

Preparing a Welcome for the Fenians

By the autumn of 1865, both the provincial press and the public had sensationalized the activities and goals of the Fenian Brotherhood and the threat they posed to New Brunswick. Lieutenant-Governor Gordon was bombarded with unsolicited information and seemingly unending advice on how to counter the danger. Unknown to the general public, Gordon and the British military authorities routinely received intelligence reports from the British diplomatic and consular services in the United States. Although the public envisaged that a full-scale Fenian invasion of New Brunswick was imminent, Gordon concluded that this was improbable. He believed the main threat to be small-scale raids across the Maine border, most likely in the form of small bands of marauders robbing and plundering frontier communities. Gordon resisted taking any action until he received an encoded message from Ambassador Bruce in Washington on Tuesday, December 5, warning of imminent Fenian action. Even then, Gordon refused to call out the volunteer militia, as that would involve major government expenditures and would adversely affect the local economy by taking militiamen away from their normal employment. Instead, Gordon conceived of forming temporary home guard units in exposed frontier communities. The home guards would be unpaid volunteers, assigned specific local tasks and would undergo weekly training sessions. Having decided on a course of action, Gordon set out to explain his plan to officials in the frontier communities.

By Tuesday evening, Gordon was in St. Stephen, having travelled overland directly from Fredericton – but not without adventure. The night before, thieves had broken into Doherty's store in Fredericton, helped themselves to the stock, including new boots, and then stole a horse and wagon from the stable. When Gordon and his entourage reached the settlement of Dunbarton, thirty-two kilometers from St. Stephen, they spotted two Irishmen named Mulherrin and Donahue nonchalantly driving a wagon and wearing new boots. Recognizing the stolen horse and wagon, Gordon's aide de camp, Captain Hallowes, immediately became a sheriff *per tempore* while two other staff were appointed special constables on the spot. They promptly arrested the two men and returned them to Fredericton for trial.

On arrival in St. Stephen, Gordon consulted with leading members of the community and the next day convened a meeting of the local magistrates and prominent citizens in Grant Hall. At the meeting, Gordon discussed the intelligence he had received, outlined the possibility of plundering raids by Fenian marauders and suggested forming a home guard of young, able-bodied men, armed and ready to act. He promised to make one hundred rifles available. He suggested that such a measure would ward off an attack, believing that the Fenians would opt to raid only undefended communities. Gordon also took the opportunity to present his concerns about intolerance dividing the community along religious lines. It was agreed to act on the lieutenant-governor's suggestion to form a home guard, and Lieutenant Colonel James A. Inches was selected to organize it.

Thanks to Colonel Inches's skill and energy, St. Stephen was well protected in the coming crisis. Inches had been promoted to major in December 1864, and within the year he was promoted again to lieutenant colonel in command of the 4th Battalion Charlotte County Militia. He was a respected resident of St. Stephen, noted for his tact and judgment. On the Saturday evening following Gordon's address, Inches enrolled 103 men into the home guard, and more enlisted later. On the

Lieutenant Colonel James Archibald Inches, the commanding officer of the 4th Battalion Charlotte County Militia and commandant of the St. Stephen garrison during the Fenian crisis. Courtesy of Valerie Teed.

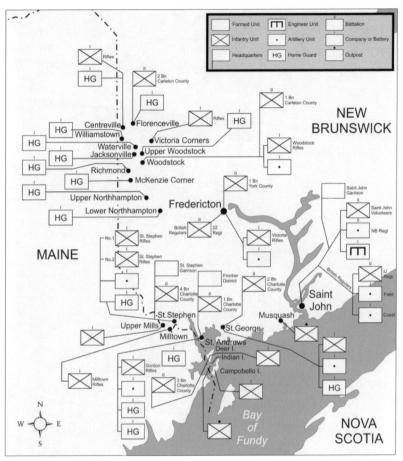

The Deployment of New Brunswick and British military forces during the Fenian Crisis, Spring, 1866. Mike Bechthold

following Monday evening, another company formed in neighbouring Milltown, with some one hundred men enrolled under Major Andrew Murchie McAdam, a participant in the 1865 Camp of Instruction. Then on Thursday, a meeting was held at Middle Landing where a third home guard company was formed under the command of Captain Francis Smith. In addition, the St. Stephen Rifle Company of the Class A militia commenced drilling nightly with full attendance. Inspired by the lieutenant-governor and under the effective leadership of Colonel Inches, a defence force had been organized along the St. Croix River within one week.

On Thursday, December 8, the lieutenant-governor was in St. Andrews convening another town meeting where he repeated the St. Stephen message. The next day, a home guard was organized under the command of Captain Robert D. James, with 109 men enrolled and divided into two companies. Two days later, a night patrol of twenty-two unarmed men commenced operations in the town. The quick response of the St. Andrews Home Guard was attributed to the leadership of Captain James, a retired captain from the British Army.

The state of the local militia was quite another matter. Lieutenant-Colonel James Boyd, the commanding officer of the 1st Battalion Charlotte County Militia, had been involved with the militia for more than twenty years and was the local elected representative in the legislative assembly. Boyd was a strongly opinionated man who appeared to thrive on controversy. He opposed the introduction of the volunteer militia and did everything possible to prevent the establishment of a Class A unit in St. Andrews. The old militia system had provided him with a great opportunity for political patronage, a prerogative he was determined to retain. A volunteer company had been organized under Major J. H. Whitlock in February 1862, but it faced Boyd's opposition. The commander-in-chief, not understanding the root cause of the dispute, disbanded Whitlock's company for unsatisfactory attendance. Thanks to Boyd's manipulation, no one from the 1st Battalion attended the 1865 Camp of Instruction. On July 17, 1865, another attempt was made to form a Class A company under Captain Edward Pheasant. Pheasant's company also failed to receive essential support from Boyd and as a result was not approved by the commander-in-chief. During his December visit to St. Andrews, Gordon learned first-hand of the disorganized state of the local militia and the dissatisfaction of its members. He directed that an investigation be conducted immediately.

On Friday afternoon, December 9, the lieutenant-governor travelled by special train from St. Andrews to Woodstock. There he convened a meeting of the magistrates in the Blanchard Hotel where he repeated the message he had already given in St. Stephen and St. Andrews. If anything, Gordon spoke even more passionately about the "danger from within" and his concern about a religious division occurring inside the province. He feared that the intolerance created by the Fenian threat could inflict "a wound on their country which neither they nor their children would see healed; sowing a bitter harvest for future generations to reap." Under the leadership of Lieutenant Colonel William Teed Baird of Woodstock and Lieutenant Colonel James Rice Tupper of Florenceville, two highly regarded community leaders, home guards were established within the week along the Carleton County border with Maine in the communities of Richmond, Upper Woodstock, Jacksontown, Centreville and Florenceville. Colonel Tupper, the commanding officer of the 2nd Battalion Carleton County Militia, reported an enthusiastic response from the men in his area, where in one day 105 men had enrolled in Centreville and sixty-two men in Florenceville. In Woodstock, two companies of home guard formed under Captains John Leary and William Lindsay. The Class A Woodstock Volunteer Rifles under Captain George Strickland received an influx of new recruits and intensified its training program. All this was achieved with the encouragement and support of Colonel Baird, a key figure in the development of the New Brunswick militia. Selected for his leadership ability, he was appointed commanding officer of the 1st Battalion Carleton County Militia in January 1863. He participated in the commissions to review the militia acts and was subsequently appointed the deputy quartermaster-general. He commanded one of the training battalions at the 1865 Camp of Instruction.

Gordon relied on able militia officers to organize local units elsewhere in the province. In Fredericton, Lieutenant Colonel the Honourable Lemuel Wilmot, commanding the 1st Battalion York County Militia, was another key figure in the development of the militia in New Brunswick. Selected for his leadership qualities, he commanded the second training battalion at the 1865 Camp of Instruction. With his encouragement and support, an effective Class A volunteer company, called the Victoria

Six officers and a private of the Saint John Volunteer Battalion circa 1863. The officer seated in the centre is believed to be the first commanding officer, Lieutenant Colonel the Honourable John Robertson. The private is reclining on the floor. NBM 6197

Rifles, was organized in Fredericton under the command of Major Edward Simond. The Fredericton militia units had the benefit of receiving support, in particular training assistance, from the British garrison stationed in the city. Because the capital city was not directly on the Maine border, it was deemed unnecessary to form home guard units.

Being the major seaport and the largest community in New Brunswick, Saint John had a large concentration of militiamen and half of the Class A volunteer units, in addition to a large British garrison. On August 12, 1863, six of the volunteer companies were combined into the Saint John Volunteer Battalion under the command of Lieutenant Colonel the Honourable John Robertson. A month later, Gordon attached Captain Thomas Anderson, a retired officer from the 78th Highland Regiment, to the battalion with the provincial rank of major. He remained with the battalion for a year enhancing its effectiveness. Although only five companies were present at the annual inspection in September 1864, there were 374 men on parade. Within months, the sixth company was reorganized, trained and back on parade under the command of Captain James R. McShane, the only officer in the battalion to attend the 1865 Camp of Instruction. The inspection of this company in December 1865 received favourable comment in the *Morning News*: "The inspection was, as it should be, rigid, the evolutions were executed with more than average precision, and the officers evinced a general acquaintance with their business." Colonel Robertson later resigned having found that he could not handle both the demands of the volunteer militia and his legislative duties. He was replaced by Major Robert W. Crookshank, who was promoted to lieutenant colonel. A year later, the adjutant general inspected each company separately and made another favourable report. He also noted the recent construction of a rifle range at Fort Howe, considering it a great asset, but highlighted the need for a proper drill hall in which to conduct battalion drill. Of the six batteries in the New Brunswick Regiment of Artillery, five were located in Saint John. The regiment's commanding officer was Lieutenant Colonel Foster, another highly esteemed militia officer. A volunteer company of engineers under the command of Captain John Hegan Parks was also located in the city. It was believed that these Class A units would provide adequate protection for Saint John against any Fenian attack.

Another effective militia officer was Lieutenant Colonel Douglas Wetmore of St. George. One of New Brunswick's first volunteer companies was formed in St. George in January 1860, and the key role it played during the visit of the Prince of Wales to Saint John was remembered with pride. Because St. George was located along the Fundy coast, its citizens felt highly exposed to a Fenian incursion, and Colonel Wetmore took the initiative in providing for the defence of his town. Two Class A volunteer companies, each of one hundred men, were organized under command of Captains James Bolton and James Bogue, and a thirty-man home guard armed with Enfield rifles was formed under Captain James O'Brien. Captain Bolton's company was uniquely armed with two cannons and a swivel gun, all privately owned by Colonel Wetmore. Sergeant Major Patrick Finnegan, a veteran of the 63rd Regiment and the Crimean War, was responsible for posting guards on all approaches to town, each consisting of two noncommissioned officers and eight privates. A two-storey blockhouse was built on Carleton Hill on property granted by Dr. Robert Thomson and with timber provided by local merchants. Commanding the approaches to St. George and manned by Captain Bolton's artillery battery, this building was called Fort Carleton.

Although there was still much to be done, by the New Year of 1866, defence measures were in place along the frontier of New Brunswick. However, the Fenian Brotherhood had also gained in strength and confidence. Their activity increased as more Fenian "circles," or lodges, organized across the United States, military companies were drilled and funds raised to support the Brotherhood. General Sweeny busied himself organizing his staff, developing his plans and preparing for a spring campaign. The British authorities believed that a "rising" was planned for both Ireland and British North America, with a target date of St. Patrick's Day 1866. The press followed developments within the Fenian Brotherhood closely, enhancing reports with speculation and exaggeration. Authorities anxiously awaited March 17, while the public fretted about the adequacy of the commander-in-chief's defence arrangements.

St. Andrews volunteer militia on parade, circa 1866, with, it is believed, Captain Henry Osborne's artillery battery in left foreground and Captain B. R. Stephenson's Gordon Rifles in right background. Courtesy of Harold Wright Collection.

Chapter Five

The St. Patrick's Day Alert

While awaiting the anticipated Fenian attack on St. Patrick's Day, Lieutenant-Governor Gordon took full advantage of the time available to improve defence arrangements and resolve problems. In these endeavours, he was ably assisted by Lieutenant Colonel George Joseph Maunsell, an ex-captain of the 15th Regiment who served as adjutant general of the New Brunswick militia. To ease Maunsell's growing work load, Lieutenant Colonel Andrew C. Otty, from the King's County Militia, was appointed deputy adjutant general. Otty was tasked "to examine" the frontier posts and report his findings directly back to Gordon. The resolution of the unsatisfactory state of the St. Andrews militia was a priority. As noted in the *St. Andrews Standard*, "The appointment of Col. Otty . . . is most opportune; the Colonel's ability and popularity as a Militia officer, will secure him a welcome, and result in the organization we hope of our 'disorganized Battalion' to use the words of one of his officers. Col. Otty 'is the right man in the right place,' and a thorough soldier."

Otty arrived in St. Andrews on December 28, 1865. After taking up quarters in the Railroad Hotel, he held discussions with Captain James and met with the home guard. The exchange between the militiamen and Otty was direct and frank. The men wanted the right to elect their officers. Otty made it clear that this would not happen, as the commander-in-chief retained the sole right to commission officers. With Colonel Boyd in mind, they asked, "will you give us a guarantee, if we do Volunteer we will not be placed under the control of a person who is decidedly obnoxious to the majority of us." Otty responded again that it was the commander-in-chief's prerogative to select the officers. The volunteers were encouraged, however, when Otty promised that any approved company would be under the direct control of Gordon, properly armed, provided with a qualified drill instructor and would not be subjected to unnecessary paperwork. Otty explained that he would not make any recommendations to Gordon until he had visited St. Stephen and Woodstock and reviewed their defence measures. Otty returned to St. Andrews on January 8. The home guard was reinstated under Captain James, and a Class A volunteer company of the active militia was approved under the command of Captain Edward Pheasant. To show their delight, members of the new company requested that they be called the Gordon Rifles.

Otty believed that a second volunteer unit could be raised in St. Andrews without detriment to the Gordon Rifles and recommended the formation of an artillery battery. By mid-January, a new battery of artillery was organized with a strength of forty-one gunners under the command of Captain Henry Osborne. This new battery became part of Colonel Foster's New Brunswick Regiment of Artillery. Although the volunteer militia and home guard had been placed on a sound footing, dissatisfaction continued in 1st Battalion Charlotte County Militia. On March 14, a public meeting was held to enrol the militia, but only nine volunteered for service because of the unpopularity of Colonel Boyd.

Otty moved on to St. Stephen where he found defence measures well advanced. The St. Stephen Volunteer Company drilled under Drill Sergeant T. Quinn of the British 10th Regiment and, as reported in the *Saint Croix Courier*, was "growing daily in numbers and efficiency." Captain T. J. Smith, the company commander, was actively involved and had finished the armory at his own expense, making it "a pleasant and inviting place to meet." Colonel Foster of the New Brunswick Regiment of Artillery and Captain William T. Rose had discussed the establishment of an artillery battery in St. Stephen. By the end of January, artillery training had commenced under the direction of Sergeant Connolly. On February 24, 1866, the lieutenant-governor inspected the St. Stephen Volunteer Rifles and was very complimentary. He is quoted in the *Saint Croix Courier* as saying "that nearly all present had only been drilling since the commencement of the winter, and he was surprised and gratified to observe the progress they had made."

The defence measures envisaged by the lieutenant-governor in Carleton County met both successes and failures. In response to Colonel Tupper's appeal, over one hundred men enrolled in the Centreville Home Guard. Some of these recruits believed that they would elect their officers and became disgruntled when Tupper appointed Captain William Dell Estey and Lieutenant Charles A. West as the company officers. In a scathing letter to the editor of the *Carleton Sentinel,* one of the recruits, Henry T. Scholey, claimed this violated his right as a Briton, and he and seventy others refused to drill. Captain Estey was quick to rebut with another letter, stating that the Centreville Home Guard still existed and was successfully parading with over thirty men. He emphasized that only the commander-in-chief had the authority to appoint officers and that poor Scholey "did not know any better, therefore the sin of ignorance in this particular case, should be winked at." Captain Estey was also quick to inform Scholey in writing that his name had been "erased" from the home guard.

There was also confusion concerning the home guard in the Town of Woodstock. Following the lieutenant-governor's appeal in mid-December, almost one hundred men enthusiastically enrolled in the guard. They then elected their officers and divided into two companies under the command of Captains John Leary and William Lindsay. Colonel Baird, however, refused to acknowledge these home guard companies with their elected officers. Instead, Baird ordered Lindsay, an ensign in the county militia, to start the process again and form a new home guard with Lindsay as an appointed officer, but he refused. Attempts to appeal directly to the commander-in-chief over the head of Colonel Baird failed. The original companies continued to drill under their elected offi-

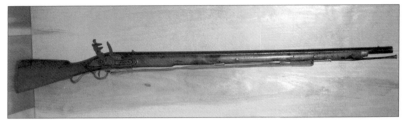

Musket carried by Private H.E. Hill of No. 1 Company, St. Stephen
Rifles, during the Fenian crisis. The musket is a New Land Pattern, light
infantry model, which came into production in 1802. The lock is marked
'Tower' and has the crown of George III. The lack of more modern arms
necessitated the use of these outdated weapons during the Fenian crisis.

cers without official sanction, leaving the status of the Woodstock Home
Guard unresolved. Despite this controversy, the Woodstock Volunteer
Rifle Company under the direction of Captain George Strickland,
Lieutenant Baird and Ensign G. E. Boyer drilled and expanded. This
Class A company received public acclaim after a fire destroyed the building housing Belyea's store and dwelling on King's Street, and Captain
Strickland, "with his usual forethought," detailed members of his com-
pany to stand guard over the exposed property. Strickland again received
public notice when it was learned that he had established a "reading
room" for the benefit of his men. In addition to the Woodstock Volunteer
Rifle Company, Colonel Baird had under his command another 302
men in home guard units located outside Woodstock. At the same time,
a Class A volunteer rifle company had been successfully raised in the
Centreville-Wicklow area under the command of Captain Issac Adams.
It held regular drill parades in the recently erected Centreville drill hall.
In training his company, Captain Adams had the benefit of having attended the 1865 Camp of Instruction. At the end of January, the *Carleton
Sentinel* reported "They certainly are a firm looking body of men, and
performed their drill well."

The defence of the City of Saint John was based on the Saint John
Volunteer Battalion and the three hundred men in the volunteer artillery

batteries. Colonel Crookshank felt he was unable to devote the necessary time and attention to the volunteer battalion at this time of crisis and requested six months' leave of absence. The vacancy was filled on January 17, 1866, with the appointment of Lieutenant Colonel Otty as the acting commanding officer. He took charge immediately, devoting all his time to his military duties. Otty set up training programs for officers and non-commissioned officers. Captain Cyprian Edward Godard raised a seventh company in the Portland district. As well, the uniquely uniformed "Zouaves" company was disbanded and replaced with a company commanded by Captain Charles Campbell. Military experience and professionalism arrived with the selection of Sergeant Thomas McKenzie of the 64th Regiment as sergeant major and Sergeant McCreary of the 2nd Queen's Own Regiment as drill instructor. Drills were held regularly and an alert system developed to assemble the battalion quickly in an emergency. In preparation for the anticipated emergency on St. Patrick's Day, Gordon called out the Saint John Volunteer Battalion on active service on March 14, with a paid strength of eighteen officers and 418 men. On the same day, Captain George H. Pick's volunteer battery of artillery, consisting of three officers and eighty-three gunners, was also called out. Both units were placed under command of Brevet-Colonel John Amber Cole, the commander of Her Majesty's troops in New Brunswick.

As St. Patrick's Day approached, public apprehension grew. On March 7, the *St. Andrews Standard*, quoting from a telegram received from New York, reported that the Fenian General Sweeny would make a demonstration against Canada "about the middle of March with a small force and strike New Brunswick via the Maine frontier with his main column." The newspaper went on to decry the lack of artillery and proper arms for the home guard. This perceived threat resulted in a run on the banks in Saint John forcing the management of the Savings Bank to seek financial support from Baring Brothers in London. Colonel Cole was sent to Saint John to take command of its defence. With little time to prepare, he swung immediately into action. He placed guards from the volunteer battalion on the magazines, armories, military storehouses and other vital points around the city. Detachments from the artillery

Two unidentified privates of the Saint John Volunteer Battalion, circa 1863.
NBM X12539

battery were stationed on Partridge Island, at Reed's Point Battery and the Carleton Martello Tower. The British regulars of the 15th Regiment stationed in Saint John were concentrated in Barrack Green, placed on alert and held in readiness to respond wherever and whenever required. When the attorney general was questioned in the legislative assembly about the measures taken to protect the province against the Fenians, the government replied that adequate steps had been put in place. Gordon, however, knew differently. When Major General Sir Charles Hastings Doyle, the commander of the British Forces in the Lower Provinces, asked what support he could expect from the provincial militia, Gordon had to admit very little was available.

The defence of the Port of Saint John received a major boost with the arrival of HMS *Pylades*. A request for a British warship to protect Saint John had been made during the panic in December, but had been rescinded. With growing concern over a Fenian incursion, the lieutenant-governor made another request on February 1. The senior naval officer in Halifax sent a warship immediately. With only one ship in port, the choice was easy: HMS *Pylades,* a 1,278-ton steam corvette with a crew of 274 men, a 20-cannon broadside and two 110-pounder Armstrong guns fore and aft was sent. Under the command of Captain Arthur W. A. Hood, it arrived in Saint John on February 6, coated in ice after a difficult winter passage. The *Pylades* was expected to remain until spring.

Following his arrival in Saint John, Captain Hood remained onboard his ship for more than a week. As Colonel Cole explained to Gordon, "he has returned from 2 years West Indies and cannot face cold . . . and it is enough to drive him into the Asylum." Less fortunate was *Pylades'* Lieutenant Pauline, who took a chill on the voyage from Halifax and after a short illness, in the era before antibiotics, died of "congestion of the lungs." On March 29, a large crowd of Saint Johners watched the spectacle of a naval funeral conducted by the ship's company, with Pauline's coffin transported on a gun carriage, a firing party and the band of the 15th Regiment playing the Death March.

Captain Hood informed Gordon that his instructions from the British Admiralty directed him to provide "any assistance you may require for

"HMS *Pylades* in a Squall," from the *Illustrated London News*, dated December 4, 1869. The *Pylades* played a major role in the Fenian crisis.

the protection of St. John from any attack that may be made on it by a band of Fenians from the United States." Hood explained that when his ship was on alert it took only two hours to raise steam in order to sail. In discussing how best to employ HMS *Pylades,* Hood suggested positioning it in Passamaquoddy Bay, where the Fenians could be intercepted departing Maine. However, he made it clear that if Gordon so directed he would remain in Saint John. In the event, HMS *Pylades* stayed in Saint John for the next two months.

By early March, the province of Canada was also in a state of alarm. Intelligence continued to indicate increasing Fenian activity and St. Patrick's Day as the likely date of attack. As a result, the adjutant general of the militia directed that ten thousand volunteers assemble for active service for a three-week period. The response was so overwhelming that fifty thousand men could have been raised, and, after further consideration, the number of men called out was increased to fourteen thousand.

As in New Brunswick, this force was deployed to watch the approaches to frontier towns and protect vital points along the border.

The long anticipated St. Patrick's Day proved to be anti-climatic. The Saint John *Morning News* reported that "the long talked of and ominous St. Patrick's Day arrived on Saturday morning, and a more mild, pleasant, genial one than it proved to be could scarcely be experienced at this early season. It came we have already said, in peace, and we have now to add that it departed in the same spirit." The *St. Andrews Standard* noted that "St. Patrick's Day passed off here in an unusually quiet manner. Not even the hard working man had his heart warmed by a swig of mountain dew. It was too quiet by half." The *Carleton Sentinel* said, "Saturday last, St. Patrick's Day, passed off very quiet in Woodstock, there being no public demonstration whatever. Many persons throughout the country were impressed with the belief that this was the day on which O'Mahoney [*sic*] with his army was to make his onslought [*sic*] on us." The Fredericton *Headquarters* reported that St. Patrick's Day passed without incident and gave credit to Gordon's defence measures for securing the peace for the province. March 17 also passed without incident in Canada. The only reported excitement was the firing of some guns and rockets across the border at Lubec, Maine. Both the lieutenant-governor and the general public, however, believed that a Fenian attack was yet to come and defence preparations continued unabated.

Major General Sir Charles Hastings Doyle, the commander of British Forces in the Lower Provinces during the Fenian crisis. PANB P360-14.

Chapter Six

Let Them Come — If They Dare

After the St. Patrick's Day scare, Lieutenant-Governor Gordon re-assessed the threat posed by the Fenian Brotherhood. He concluded that a major invasion across the Maine border was unlikely and, assuming the continued presence of the Royal Navy in the Bay of Fundy, so was an attack on Saint John. Gordon believed that an attempt by the Fenians to seize either an island in the Passamaquoddy Bay or some location near St. Andrews was still conceivable, but a series of raids across the Maine border remained the most likely possibility. Since the British regulars stationed in New Brunswick formed ready reserves in Fredericton and Saint John, it followed that the defence of the frontier must rest primarily upon the provincial militia.

In developing a plan, Gordon turned for advice to General Doyle, the British commander-in-chief in the Lower Provinces. In the discussions that followed, it quickly became apparent that Gordon, the public servant, and Doyle, the professional soldier, had widely differing views on defence. Doyle, a veteran of the Crimean War, saw a thousand kilometers of border to defend, including a number of isolated islands. Based on his extensive experience, Doyle knew this was an impossible task, particularly when taking into account the limited military resources available. Not all approaches across the Maine border could be protected, and those covered could not be adequately defended. The conventional military solution for such a defence problem was to concentrate military resources well back in a central location, wait for the enemy to attack and then deliver a counter-stroke against the flanks and rear of the invading columns. The suggestion that they abandon the frontier communities was totally unacceptable to the lieutenant-governor. He firmly believed it would be morally wrong to yield territory to the Fenians, and he knew the provincial government would reject such a plan outright. The people in the frontier region would feel betrayed, particularly after having wholeheartedly supported Gordon's recent defence initiatives. It would prove detrimental to public support for the militia and disastrous for recruiting. Gordon also argued that the capture and occupation of a frontier community would be a major psychological victory for the Fenians, providing them with a tremendous boost to their cause, recruiting and fundraising. In the end, the military commander acquiesced to the civil leader and Gordon's point of view prevailed.

The next step taken by the lieutenant-governor was to ensure he had the support of the legislative assembly. Gordon informed the house that it may be necessary "to call out a portion of the Provincial Militia Force to co-operate with Her Majesty's Regular Troops in New Brunswick." He wanted to be "in the firm confidence that any measures needful for the protection of the Province from marauding bands will meet with the most hearty concurrence and support of the Legislature and Loyal people of New Brunswick." The militia budget for 1865 had been $30,000, and in 1866 the amount budgeted was $40,000, with the increment to cover additional volunteers and an increase to allowances. Gordon explained that "the amount of extraordinary expenditure to be incurred in measures of precaution, it is of course, difficult to estimate, as it must mainly depend" on the length of time the emergency lasts. Gordon suggested the legislature be prepared to spend an additional $30,000 to $50,000. The legislative assembly readily gave the support that Gordon sought by unanimously passing the resolution, "that the House, representing the whole people of the Province, will provide for all precautionary measures that the Executive Government may deem necessary in the present emergency for the defence of the country." Despite stringent measures

Brevet Colonel John Amber Cole, the commander of British troops and provincial militia on active service in New Brunswick during the Fenian crisis. PANB P272-621

to control expenditures, the total cost of the emergency to the province of New Brunswick would amount to a staggering $112,000.

The senior military officer in New Brunswick, Brevet Colonel John Amber Cole of the 15th Regiment, had under his direct command all British troops stationed in New Brunswick and all units of the provincial militia called out on active service. Commanding officers on call-out received their orders from Colonel Cole, or officers appointed by him, except for matters of pay and promotion, which were the purview of Lieutenant Colonel Maunsell, adjutant general of militia. Those on active service were subject to the *Articles of War*, the act that provided for punishing mutiny and desertion, and all other laws applicable to British regular soldiers.

The Western Military District, located along the Maine border, was the area of greatest concern. The lieutenant-governor appointed Captain Thomas Anderson as district commander effective March 14, 1866, with the New Brunswick militia rank of lieutenant colonel. Anderson had extensive military experience, including service with the 78th Highland Regiment during the Indian Mutiny. Upon retiring from the British Army, he was assigned to the Saint John Volunteer Battalion for a year and then appointed adjutant general of the New Brunswick Militia. He was instrumental in drafting the *Militia Act* of 1865 and was a strong advocate for the establishment of camps of instruction. He was highly regarded as an experienced professional soldier. Within a day of his appointment, the *St. Andrews Standard* reported "We learn that our respected friend, Lt. Col. Anderson will visit this country for the purpose of placing the Militia in an effective state — may be on a war footing. The Colonel is so well adapted for the duty, not only from his professional knowledge and experience, but also from his great popularity, that we augur much good from his visit. He will be well received by the officers and men of the Volunteers and Militia."

The written instructions provided to Anderson gave him extraordinary scope and authority, a reflection of Gordon's confidence in him. All four battalions of the Charlotte County Militia and the two battalions of the Carleton County Militia were placed under his command. Colonel Foster was directed to place at his disposal any 3-pounder guns that he might request. The quartermaster general was directed to fill all Anderson's requisitions for arms and ammunition. Upon receiving his instructions, he was ordered to leave the next day for Saint John and Campobello. In Saint John, he was to "take an opportunity of communicating fully with Colonel Cole," his immediate military superior. The instruction further directed that "Colonel Anderson will report with as little delay as possible the nature of the steps which in his opinion would be best calculated to prevent the landing of a small hostile force in Campobello or St. Andrews & their occupation of those points. Whilst waiting for instructions on this report he will proceed to carry out his views so far as the resources at his disposal permit." Finally, Anderson was to report directly to the lieutenant-governor and "to do so frequently and fully." Anderson's appointment as district commander inspired confidence just when it was most needed, and he had the authority to act decisively. On March 17, the *Saint Croix Courier* reported "The militia force along the frontier has been placed under his command. The country is safe."

As ordered, Anderson met with Cole in Saint John and then took the steamer *New Brunswick* on its regular run to Eastport, arriving on March 15. From there he made his way to Campobello where he remained for over a week, delayed by both illness and the weather. The militia on the Passamaquoddy islands formed the 3rd Battalion Charlotte County Militia, with its headquarters on Deer Island, under the command of Lieutenant Colonel James Brown. The senior militiaman on Campobello Island was Captain Robinson. Defence measures on the island had begun prior to the arrival of Anderson. A volunteer rifle company had been formed under command of Captain Luke Bryon. This Class A company usually drilled twice weekly, but during the week of March 16, it drilled daily under the recently promoted Captain John Farmer, the battalion adjutant. A guard consisting of a sergeant and seven privates stood to nightly. Anderson found the guard armed, but without ammunition. He immediately sent his aide D'Arcy to procure a supply from St. Andrews. When he returned a couple of days later with a "keg of ammunition," the volunteers began firing practice on the rifle range. Permission was granted to call out Captain Bryon's company effective March 21. A request was made for twenty more rifles, as there were volunteers ready to carry them. In his report to Gordon, Anderson commented favourably on the excellent conduct of the volunteer company and singled out Sergeant Templeton for his zeal in command of the night guard. Steps were also taken to organize two volunteer companies on Deer Island under command of Captains Grew and Lloyd. Colonel

Anderson noted that these protective measures and his visit had calmed public fear of a Fenian invasion, which had earlier lead to some families fleeing Campobello. In a confidential letter to Gordon, Anderson praised Captain Robinson for his professional assistance, local knowledge and hospitality. Anderson's greatest concern was the lack of direct communication between St. Andrews and Campobello. If Campobello was attacked, it would take time for the information to reach St. Andrews and to provide assistance to the island.

Meanwhile, the citizens of St. Andrews were in a great state of alarm and some families were preparing to leave. The March 14 issue of the *St. Andrews Standard* noted, "Up to the present we confess very little has been accomplished. Men are ready to volunteer, provided they have rifles and ammunition." When D'Arcy returned to Campobello, he gave Anderson an unsettling account of the situation in the town. Anderson reacted by warning Colonel Inches in St. Stephen to be prepared to come to the assistance of St. Andrews and gave serious consideration to bringing in the Fredericton artillery battery with their two 6-pounders. Anderson telegraphed Gordon from Campobello requesting permission to embody Captain Pheasant's company and Captain Osborne's artillery battery, if necessary. He was reluctant to embody the battery because it was composed mainly of men employed on the railway and calling them out could adversely affect railway operations just at the time when they would be most needed.

Another key appointment made by the commander-in-chief was the selection of Major Cuthbert Willis as Commandant of St. Andrews with the local rank of lieutenant colonel. After Willis retired from the 15th Regiment, he was employed as the brigade major at the 1865 Camp of Instruction and was the inspecting officer of the Eastern District. The *St. Andrews Standard* was delighted with Willis' selection and announced that the ranks of the home guard would be filled without delay now that there was "an assurance that they will not be compelled to serve under Col. Boyd." The newspaper followed with disparaging remarks about "poor gallant Col. Boyd!" Not surprisingly, Boyd was not pleased with either Willis' appointment or the public response. He attempted a rebuttal on the floor of the legislative assembly. He claimed that he was a popular officer within his battalion and that the lieutenant-governor had asked him to take command first, but that his legislative duties precluded it. Boyd's protestations only sparked further derisive comments. A letter to the editor signed by "One of the Minions" said that Boyd's rebuttal was "a piece of egoism on his part rarely surpassed" and went on to question how Boyd could have the gall to remain in office, having had his advice ignored and passed over for command. Anderson confirmed publicly that Willis commanded the 1st Battalion Charlotte County Militia; however, he found it necessary to "send for the editor and caution him" about his libelous comments concerning Boyd. Colonel Willis set out immediately for St. Andrews to assume his new appointment. When questioned by the home guard, Willis explained that he was there only temporarily and that he could not guarantee that Boyd would not command again. Boyd was a man who knew how to carry a grudge. Later, when asked to contribute to the Victoria Day celebrations in St. Andrews, he refused. As reported in the *Saint Croix Courier* "Col James Boyd refused to subscribe a cent to buy gunpowder for firing a salute on the Queen's birthday. This the same Mr. Boyd who is at present soliciting the vote of the loyal electors of Charlotte county for a seat in the House of Assembly." Despite the stress it caused Boyd, it appeared Gordon had made a wise choice in selecting Willis.

The arrival of Colonel Willis in St. Andrews was well received by the *St. Andrews Standard.* It proclaimed, "There appears at last a spark of life in the Militia authorities." Willis took charge immediately. He found that Captain Pheasant's Gordon Rifles drilled regularly under Drill Instructor Sergeant Quinn and Captain Osborne's artillery battery mounted guard nightly. On March 21 the Gordon Rifles were embodied with the strength of three officers, three sergeants, two corporals, one bugler and twenty-six privates. They commenced garrison duties immediately. Willis established an outpost at Joe's Point Blockhouse, consisting of a sergeant, corporal and six men. This old blockhouse from the War of 1812 was located on the St. Croix River a mile from St. Andrews, opposite Robbinston, Maine, overlooking the river and the Maine border. The

Believed to be the Gordon Rifles, the St. Andrews Class A Volunteer militia company under the command of Captain Benjamin R. Stephenson, circa 1866. Courtesy of Charlotte County Archives P69-436

sergeant could raise an alarm by flying a "danger flag" by day or by dispatching a mounted messenger by night. A sergeant and six gunners from Osborne's battery were also embodied and stationed in Fort Tipperary, an old fortification dating from 1808, located at the edge of town. The home guard was reconstituted, and Captain James was appointed major of the guard. The guard was divided into two companies, each under the command of a captain and a subaltern. Noncommissioned officers were assigned and drill was conducted four times a week under qualified drill instructors. Eighty-three men volunteered for service, and within a week they provided a piquet of one sergeant and six privates to stand guard over the arms stored at the Town Hall.

When Anderson arrived in St. Andrews from Campobello, he approved all the actions taken by Willis. In addition, he had a 9-pounder cannon put into working order and placed in Market Square where it could sweep the approaches along the streets in three directions. Although he had managed to obtain several rounds of cannister, he confessed it was mainly for show, as he doubted the old cannon could be fired more than once. Anderson and Willis set out together to inspect all the outposts around the town but were hindered by the heaviest snow-fall of the winter, which had been plaguing the region for several days. Although the *St. Andrews Standard* reported "there are now excellent traveling" conditions, they became stuck in a snowdrift and broke the traces on their sled. In a confidential report to Gordon, Anderson informed him that Major James had been "most active and zealous . . . as he is a man of property his presence here is worth a good deal at present." He believed that James owned half the town by mortgage and requested permission to "retain him at any price." On March 27, Anderson was able to report with satisfaction that the people of St. Andrews seemed to be over their fright. This view was supported next day in the *St. Andrews Standard*, which stated, "The military ardor of the inhabitants cannot be excelled. Capt Pheasant's company are doing garrison duty, in martial style. Red coats in the streets are quite refreshing and the uniforms in the churches on Sabbath last, gave proof that loyalty was at a premium." The newspaper knew where to place the credit: "In fact everything is being done in a systematic and military style, which goes to prove the wisdom of Col. Anderson's appointment, and his ability, energy and popularity."

On March 28, Anderson reported to Gordon that there was a Fenian spy in St. Andrews. According to Anderson, David Barry, an American citizen, had arrived in town from Eastport and made inquiries about local defence arrangements. At one point, he bragged that he was a Fenian and that they would soon invade and he would be among them. Although uncertain about his civil powers, Anderson ordered Colonel Willis to arrest him. Once he was turned over to the civil authorities, Barry was soon released by the attorney general. The *Eastport Sentinel* was incensed by his arrest and reported quite a different story. According to the *Sentinel*, Barry, who was from Concord, New Hampshire, had returned to Eastport to close his business and visit old friends after having moved away. While visiting and having dinner in St. Andrews, "the subject of a Fenian invasion was discussed, and Mr. Barry in reply to a question expressed the opinion that 60,000 Fenians could take the Canadas. Soon after dinner Mr. Barry was arrested and brought before a Justice Fitzgerald, who ordered him to be committed to jail on the charge of be-

Joe's Point Blockhouse overlooking the St. Croix River near St. Andrews. Built during the War of 1812 and used as an outpost during the Fenian crisis. PANB P23-20

ing guilty of treason." Barry was lodged in "a filthy loathsome dungeon" in "a cell reserved for murderers," denied bail, and released only after a lawyer was finally obtained.

Barry was not the first to be arrested for treason. Captain Robinson on Campobello Island arrested Hugh Muldoon of Eastport, formerly of Saint John. He too had been sent to St. Andrews, held in jail and then released. It was later determined that Muldoon was indeed a Fenian. Robinson maintained that there were other suspicious characters on the island and requested handcuffs be forwarded to him without delay. The ever energetic Anderson, not pleased with the reaction of the civil authorities, threatened to take matters into his own hands, if necessary, by taking a "clerk of the Peace out with me to read the Riot Act."

With the defence of the Frontier District in the capable hands of Anderson, Colonel Cole concentrated his attention on the security of Saint John. His first concern was the safety of the arms and ammunition scattered in various locations around the city. The arms allotted to the militia were moved to a storage space under the Saint John Volunteer

Fort Tipperary, St. Andrews built in 1808 during the Napoleonic Wars. PANB

Battalion orderly room, which was manned twenty-four hours a day. It took several horse-drawn wagons a whole day to move the seventy-eight boxes of arms. The ammunition stored in the Carleton Martello Tower and at Fort Howe was moved to a secure location in town. Cole and his engineer officer made a thorough inspection of all the defensive positions around the city. He instructed the engineers to prepare the Martello tower for defence by removing the roof and mounting cannon. The volunteer artillery batteries occupied Reed's Point Battery and established sentry posts at what was later known as Fort Dufferin and at Sand Cove. Fifty artillerymen from Captain Pick's battery boarded a tug and landed on Partridge Island, along with a supply of arms, ammunition, stoves, bedding, baggage and provisions. Unfortunately, the engineer work necessary to complete these tasks was delayed by severe winter weather, which, Cole noted, was "too boisterous to work."

On March 19, Cole inspected the Saint John Volunteer Battalion and reported 206 effective men and 186 recruits on parade. The battalion commenced daily drills lasting five to six hours at the Reed's Point Wharf. Because of the lack of accommodation, he accepted Colonel Otty's recommendation that one hundred men be quartered in the barracks and the remainder be allowed to return home at night. To improve the administration of the Volunteer Battalion, Acting Major D. Wilson, a secretary to Gordon and captain in the York Volunteers, was selected

Carleton Martello Tower seen from an adjacent hill showing the battery position built during the Fenian crisis. NBM 1956-43-11

to temporarily replace Major Charles R. Ray, who was absent on leave in England. The Volunteer Battalion was ordered to conduct patrols in the city and establish an outpost at Musquash, consisting of a sergeant and eight privates. This outpost covered the land approach to the city from the west and was positioned to give early warning of an attack.

Cole informed the lieutenant-governor that the public remained fearful and that some people's actions were "ludicrous." For example, a family at Red Head never lit a candle at night for fear of drawing cannon fire from a marauding Fenian ship, and "some Ladies put 3 dresses on at night - so as to carry what is dear to them into the woods - in case of flight." Cole believed the civil authorities needed strengthening in order to be ready to suppress any local unrest. When Police Magistrate Tapley requested twelve carbines, Cole replied that if arms could not be obtained from the militia quartermaster, he would provide them, but suggested pistols would be a better choice than carbines. To assess the situation for himself, Gordon arrived in Saint John on Friday, March 23, to spend the weekend. He stayed at the Stubb's Hotel, where the volunteer battalion mounted guard for his protection. On Saturday, the lieutenant-governor reviewed the volunteer battalion at Barrack Green, where he gave a stirring address outlining the Fenian threat and explaining why the battalion had been called out on active service. However, not everyone agreed with the lieutenant-governor. On March 28, the *Morning News* said, "We are of opinion that the Government have done real harm, unmixed with the slightest gain of good, in their recent and ill-timed mandate, calling out the Volunteers. The effect has been to take men away from their avocations, and thus cripple shipyards, foundries and mills in the commencement of the season."

Considering that it was only at the end of December 1865 that the lieutenant-governor started taking measures to protect against the Fenians, a great deal had been accomplished in three months. An effective command structure was in place, government funding arranged and a thousand men of the provincial militia stood ready along the Maine border from Centreville in Carleton County, south to St. Andrews and along the Bay of Fundy to Saint John. Although there was much left to be done to increase the effectiveness of this provincial field force, New Brunswick was significantly more prepared for any Fenian action than it had been. To quote the Saint John *Morning News* in discussing the Fenian Brotherhood, "Let them come, if they dare."

Chapter Seven

The Fenians Are Among Us

We are the Fenian Brotherhood, skilled in the arts of war,
And we're going to fight for Ireland, the land that we adore.
Many battles we have won, along with the boys in blue,
And we'll go and capture Canada, for we've nothing else to do.
— A popular Fenian song

After months of speeches, parades and donating their hard earned money
to the cause, the membership of the Fenian Brotherhood clamoured for
action. The O'Mahony wing of the Brotherhood had no option but to
put its plans into motion. On St. Patrick's Day 1866, the Fenian leadership approved Bernard Doran Killian's proposal to invade Campobello
Island in the belief that occupying a piece of British territory would give
the Fenians a belligerent status under international law. They could then
issue letters of marque and reprisal to privateers to prey on British shipping, purchase arms and ammunition freely, and raise an army without breaking any American laws or violating neutrality. Unfortunately
for the enterprise, no attempt was made to keep the decision to invade
Campobello a secret. Charles W. Beckwith of Fredericton was attend-
ing Harvard University in Boston when a former Frederictonian, Jack
O'Brien, a Fenian leader, invited him to a rally. There the proposal to
invade Campobello was openly discussed. Without delay, Beckwith fore-

warned New Brunswick authorities. As usual, British spies were omnipresent and also provided detailed reports.

Once Killian received approval, preparations were set in motion. Since sending an armed body of men to the Maine border would violate American law, it was decided that the men and the arms would travel separately. The Fenians hired the schooner *Ocean Spray* in New York and loaded it with military stores, including a consignment of Spencer rifles. Concurrently, the Fenian rank and file began making their way to the Maine border in small contingents taking separate routes. Although they frequently referred to themselves as "delegates," they made little effort to conceal their identity, as most wore parts of uniform and almost all sported knives and revolvers.

In mid-March 1866, the *Eastport Sentinel* noted that "our New Brunswick neighbours along the line are greatly excited by the apprehension of an invasion by the Fenians. We are of the opinion that this organization which is causing so much excitement in this country and in England and Ireland, will strike a blow somewhere soon. The excitement cannot be sustained much longer without action." On April 11, the *Eastport Sentinel* announced, "The Fenians are indeed among us." A day earlier, Robert Ker, the British Vice Consul in Eastport, sent a telegram informing Colonel Willis in St. Andrews that one hundred unarmed Fenians had arrived and that their arms had been delayed in Portland by American authorities. The Saint John *Morning News* enlarged on this report stating, "There were many startling rumors about in City yesterday respecting movements of the Fenian banditti. It was said that upwards of two hundred armed men endeavored to take passage on board the American boat at Portland for Eastport, but were refused passage unless they left their arms behind them, and that a few men remained to superintend the transportation of the arms, while the others proceeded to, and landed at, Eastport." Other reports warned that groups of Fenians were approaching Eastport from different directions, intending to make it the starting point for an attack on New Brunswick.

On April 10, General Killian and three aides arrived in Eastport by steamer where they spent the first couple of days securing financing from

"Eastport, Maine The Rendezvous of the Fenians in the United States."
Illustrated London News, 5 May 1866. New Brunswick Museum.

New York. Once funds became available, a series of mysterious and confusing activities occurred in and around Eastport: Colonel Favor's swivel gun disappeared, but he later received payment for the weapon from persons unknown; reports circulated that the nearby Pembroke Iron Works had been contracted to recast several old cannons; three large kegs of powder were purchased and men were set to work making cartridges; Killian rented Trescott Hall in Eastport for a convention, which also became his headquarters; Vice Consul Ker telegraphed Colonel Anderson that two schooners had been engaged, one to sail to Lubec for arms and the other to go to Machias. The stories and rumours circulating about the Fenians were so confusing that David Main, the editor of the *Saint Croix Courier* in St. Stephen, went to Eastport to obtain first-hand information and checked into the hotel where the Fenian leaders were staying. Breakfast there provided an excellent opportunity to observe the "enemy." He described Killian as "a fine portly looking fellow, broad open countenance, but with rather a sinister expression of the eye. He is accompanied by two secretaries, one of whom is a genteel, modest looking individual with no particular distinguishing features, the other one named McDermott is a rough Irish lad, evidently lacking in brains, judgment and experience, as quiet as a mouse in the presence of his master, but garrulous and bombastic when the latter is out of sight."

The Fenians continued to arrive in Eastport and along the St. Croix River by boat, stagecoach and on foot. While awaiting the arrival of their arms, they drilled on the sandy beach near Dog Island at Eastport and at Robbinston on the St. Croix River without any interference from American authorities. Because they moved in small groups and never concentrated, it was difficult to determine precisely how many Fenians appeared in Maine; however, at peak strength it is believed they numbered about one thousand. Vice Consul Ker estimated four hundred in Eastport, four hundred in Calais and another two hundred scattered between Lubec, Pembroke and Robbinston.

Not surprisingly, the arrival of the Fenians increased tension in New Brunswick; it also created considerable apprehension on the Maine side of the border. Washington Long, Collector of Customs in Eastport, telegraphed the Treasury Department to urgently request an experienced officer be sent to take command. On the same day, Lieutenant-Governor Gordon telegraphed Secretary of State William Seward, informing him of the imminent arrival of the *Ocean Spray* loaded with arms. The American government's concern grew, both for the safety of their citizens facing armed strangers roaming their communities and for the threat posed to their neutrality. This pressure forced Washington to abandon its complacent and ambivalent attitude toward the Fenian Brotherhood. Commissioner L. G. Downes and Deputy Marshal B. F. Farrar were sent to Eastport to ensure that the neutrality of the United States was not compromised. Seward notified Attorney General James Speed of the situation along the Maine border and requested he take appropriate action. The United States Navy formed a strong squadron for duty in eastern waters under the command of Acting Rear Admiral Boggs, consisting of the 9-gun side-wheel steamer USS *De Soto,* the 4-gun double-ender ironclad USS *Mantonomak,* the 7-gun side-wheel steamer USS *Augusta*, the 9-gun double-ender USS *Winooski* and the 7-gun USS

USS *Winooski*. Built in Boston and commissioned in June 1865. She was employed in Maine waters during the Fenian crisis, where three of her crew won the Congressional Medal of Honour for bravery while saving two sailors from drowning. Courtesy of U.S. Naval Historical Center NH 43863

Don. This Eastern Squadron was ordered to rendezvous at Eastport by April 30 and remain until the "Fenian excitement" had abated. In response to Collector Long's request, the Secretary of War ordered Major General George Gordon Meade, the hero of the Battle of Gettysburg, to Eastport.

Meanwhile, Fenian activity continued to increase along the border. The steamer SS *Queen* landed thirty to forty Fenians wearing sidearms at Robbinston. The other passengers on the steamer quoted the Fenians as saying that they intended to take possession of the province, raise their flag and proclaim an Irish Republic. In the dead of night, on Friday, April 13, two boatloads of men led by Dennis Doyle, the head of the Fenian circle in Calais, crossed the St. Croix River. They landed at Porter's Farm, just below St. Stephen, and were spotted by "Old Joe" Young, a well-known local character. Not unlike the famous Paul Revere, Young jumped upon his horse to spread the alarm. The thundering of hooves, the pounding on doors and the shouting of "Arm yourselves! The Fenians are upon you!" would be long remembered by the local residents. Doyle and his men contented themselves with firing a few shots in the air, setting fire to some woodpiles and returning to Maine. However, this demonstration was sufficient to frighten some residents into packing up their valuables, closing up their homes and fleeing. On the following night, Saturday, April 14, the infamous Indian Island "flag incident" occurred. As reported in the Saint John *Morning Freeman*, several strange and unusual happenings took place that day, "About 9 o'clock . . . a steamer of strange appearance passed by here [Eastport] from the Eastern passage. She came up slowly until about opposite the town, and then run up a green and red light, in place of the white one which she carried. This done, she passed on towards Lubec, anchoring opposite Friar's Head, Campobello. She stopped there about an hour and a half, and then proceeded seaward past Lubec." At about midnight, nine armed men debarked from the "steamer of strange appearance" and rowed ashore with muffled oars. They demanded at gun point that Customs Collector Dixon surrender his Union Jack. On the same night, another unusual incident occurred off Partridge Island in Saint John Harbour. At about ten o'clock in the evening, a "bright white flash [*sic*] Light was shown in the Eastern Channel about half way up the Island." Captain Pick reported that neither he nor any of the sentries could discern a ship, but that the light moved quickly around the island, flashed at intervals, disappeared and then reappeared again at midnight. The Partridge Island detachment firmly believed it was a small Fenian steamer conducting a reconnaissance. The ever vigilant Vice Consul Ker had heard that a small British schooner had been purchased in Eastport, and his suspicions were further aroused when some of the Fenians leaders were seen onboard. These events increased the speculation and uncertainty.

The long awaited *Ocean Spray* docked in Eastport on April 17, with the 129 cases of arms onboard consigned to Colonel James Kerrigan, one of Killian's lieutenants. On orders from Customs Collector Long, it was immediately detained by the captain of the revenue cutter USS *Ashuelot*. Long telegraphed the district attorney in Portland asking for further instructions. The district attorney informed Long that there were no grounds for seizure of either the vessel or arms, unless he had evidence the arms were destined for foreign territory. The Fenians may have pulled strings, leaving Long with no choice but to release the *Ocean Spray* and its cargo. However, to the chagrin of the Fenians, USS *Winooski* arrived in harbour. Its captain seized the initiative and impounded the ship and arms again, then sought direction from the secretary of the navy. Vice Consul Ker telegraphed the British ambassador in Washington requesting his intervention with the American government. He then visited Commander Cooper, the captain of the *Winooski,* to elicit his cooperation in keeping the weapons out of Fenian hands. Cooper's telegram created a serious dilemma for government officials, who had to uphold American neutrality but did not want to appear too direct as the midterm congressional elections were fast approaching and the Irish vote remained an important consideration. No one in government was willing to commit himself. While they dithered, secretary of the treasury, Hugh McCullough, instructed Long to detain the ship and arms until further notice. The next day, General Meade arrived in Eastport. After consultation with Long, the arms were removed from the *Ocean Spray* and deposited in Eastport's Fort Sullivan for safekeeping. In the process of unloading, it was learned that seven cases of rifles had disappeared. The Fenians were perplexed by this turn of events and felt betrayed by the United States government. Ker later reported that *Ocean Spray's* cargo contained more than six hundred stands of arms, 197,000 rounds of ammunition and several coehorns. Although not obvious at the time, the seizure of *Ocean Spray's* cargo of arms ended any possibility of a large-scale Fenian invasion of New Brunswick.

While the events surrounding the *Ocean Spray* were unfolding, the Fenians remained active along the border. Placards had been placed announcing a Fenian rally on April 16 in the St. Croix Hall in Calais. It was attended by a thousand people and addressed by Killian and his former New Brunswick lieutenant, Patrick A. Sinnott. Both disclaimed any intent to invade New Brunswick and confirmed that American laws would be respected. They claimed that 150,000 Irishmen had given their lives in the Civil War and that the United States owed a debt of gratitude that could be settled by supporting the Fenian Brotherhood in their goal of freeing Ireland. They announced that they would not allow Great Britain to "force" Confederation on the provinces and that the Fenian "convention" intended to remain on the border until the Confederation issue had been settled. Out of curiosity, some ladies from St. Stephen attended and reported that Killian had a "pleasant voice and a smooth fluent way of speaking." The audience was attentive but not enthusiastic.

Killian and his party remained in Calais for several days, and they took the opportunity to stroll across the international bridge to St. Stephen. Much to the annoyance of Colonel Inches, nothing could be done to stop them as long as they remained peaceful. Not to be outdone, some of the militiamen crossed over into Calais in their scarlet uniforms. These visits led to heated discussions and, on more than one occasion, fist fights followed with both sides claiming victory. To keep nerves on edge, Doyle, the Calais Fenian leader, had woodpiles built along the St. Croix River from the lower wharf in Calais to Milltown four miles away. One night, on a signal, the bonfires were set alight and guns fired. Panic ensued, and many in St. Stephen, fearing the invasion had started, fled their homes.

In Eastport on April 28, about fifty men under command of a Colonel Kelly boarded the British-owned schooner *Two Friends*. Captain Corson and his vessel had been hired earlier by Killian at ten dollars a day to be ready at a moment's notice to transport men and supplies. When Corson saw his passengers had several cases of rifles, he refused to move. At gun point, he was ordered to sail for Campobello. On the way past Lubec, the *Two Friends* was becalmed, and Mr. Harmon, the deputy collector of customs, managed to board the vessel. When he found armed men onboard, he quickly returned to Lubec and sounded the alert. Admiral Boggs ordered a couple of ships in pursuit. Before the American warships could sail, the *Two Friends* got under way, rounded a point of land and disappeared. At that moment, the schooner *Wentworth* from Windsor, Nova Scotia, under command of Captain McBlume, hove into sight. The Fenians forced Captain Corson to pull alongside the unsuspecting *Wentworth* so that she could be boarded and seized. When everyone was safely transferred to the *Wentworth,* the *Two Friends* was scuttled. When

St. Croix River waterfront at Calais, Maine. PANB P11-109

the pursuers finally approached, they were blithely told their quarry was around the next point of land. USS *Winooski* cruised the area for a day but found nothing. The Fenians sailed back to Eastport, disembarked and discarded their ammunition, which was recovered later by local residents. Captain McBlume reported that the Fenians acted in an orderly manner and did no damage to his ship or crew. After the Fenians had left, the captain resumed command of his ship and proceeded on his voyage to New York. These acts of terrorism, however, could not be ignored by the authorities in either New Brunswick or Great Britain.

"HMS *Rosario* overhauling the Slaver *Carl*" in 1871. The *Rosario* exemplified the world-wide commitment of the Royal Navy. It helped end a rebellion in Jamaica in 1865, participated in the Fenian crisis in 1866 and then sailed to the South Pacific to suppress the slave trade. <small>Courtesy of National Library of Australia</small>

Chapter Eight

Imperial Military Might

In April 1866, the Fenians mustered along the Maine border. Intelligence reports indicated that their numbers could reach between two to three thousand men, some armed with modern repeating Spencer rifles, and supported by artillery. Lieutenant-Governor Gordon recognized that the small volunteer force that he had organized to protect New Brunswick would be inadequate to repel a Fenian attack of such magnitude. He therefore turned to Great Britain for assistance. The insult to the British flag by the Fenian raiders at the Indian Island Customs House gave impetus to the British response.

The Royal Navy was first to react. The 21-gun HM Steam Corvette *Pylades* had been in Saint John since February 8, providing protection to the harbour. On April 9, *Pylades* hoisted anchor and sailed for St. Andrews. There, Captain Hood conferred with Colonel Anderson, and then on April 11, the *Pylades* took station off Welshpool on Campobello Island. The day *Pylades* left, HM Steam Sloop *Rosario* arrived in St. Andrews. The 673-ton *Rosario* had a crew of 160 and was armed with eleven guns. For the next two weeks, she operated on the St. Croix River, taking station off either Robbinston or Navy Island to secure the seaward approaches to St. Andrews. The presence of these two British warships made a Fenian invasion of either Campobello Island or St. Andrews a gamble.

Halifax was the summer and fall base for the North American and West Indies Squadron of the Royal Navy, which normally consisted of some thirty ships. For the last two years, the commander of the squadron had been Vice Admiral Sir James Hope. He had played a key role in the unsuccessful joint French and British expedition against China in the Second Opium War. In the fierce fighting along the Peiho River, he had been seriously wounded, losing part of his hip and a leg, but that had not hindered his career as a naval officer. During the winter of 1865-66, Hope and his squadron had been involved in suppressing an insurrection in Jamaica. On Sunday, April 8, Hope sailed into Halifax onboard his flagship HMS *Duncan,* where he was quickly apprised of the situation on the Maine border. Gordon telegraphed Hope saying, "I consider the presence of another war steamer if possible with Marines on board urgently required in Passamaquoddy Bay." Hope did much better than requested. The 1,072-ton HM Steam Corvette *Niger,* with a crew of 160 and thirteen guns, was ordered to Saint John and arrived on April 13. On April 19, the 571-ton HM Steam Sloop *Cordelia* with a crew of 130 men and eleven guns arrived in the Bay of Fundy. The 751-ton HM Steam Sloop *Fawn* with 160 men and seventeen guns reached Saint John on April 20 and five days later was in St. Andrews. Meanwhile, Admiral Hope sailed from Halifax on HMS *Duncan* and arrived at St. Andrews on April 17. The three-deck *Duncan* was the largest and last wooden British warship to be built, the culmination of two hundred years of warship design. Launched in 1859, she weighed 5,720 tons, was 252 feet long, had a draught of 25 feet 8 inches and was equipped with 800-horsepower engines. Her crew consisted of 49 officers, 701 seamen and 150 marines. She was armed with eighty-one cannons, with modern Armstrong guns on her upper deck, including a 110-pounder. By the third week of April 1866, the Royal Navy had an overwhelming presence in the Bay of Fundy.

During this period, about ten thousand regular British soldiers were stationed throughout British North America, of which 3,500 served in the Maritime provinces under the commander of the British Forces in the Lower Provinces, General Doyle, whose headquarters was located

The 81-gun HMS *Duncan* the flagship of Vice Admiral Sir James Hope, at Halifax in 1865. Courtesy of the Maritime Museum of the Atlantic MP67.24.1

in Halifax. The Halifax garrison consisted of Royal Artillery and Royal Engineer units employed in manning the fortifications, plus two battalions of infantry and elements of a third. Another battalion of infantry and two artillery batteries located in New Brunswick as well as two companies of infantry in Charlottetown, P.E.I., were also under Doyle's command. Having been in North America for five years, the 15th Regiment stationed in New Brunswick had orders to rotate to Bermuda in the third week of April; it would be replaced by the 1st Battalion, 22nd Regiment coming from Malta. The imminent departure of the 15th Regiment was regretted; as the Saint John *Morning News* recorded, "We shall regret the absence of this Regiment which has earned golden opinion while stationed here. Colonels Cole and Grierson have been most popular officers, and have spared no exertions to make their stay here pleasant to our citizens . . . wherever the 15th Regt is stationed, it will always be most kindly remembered by the citizens of St. John."

With the growing Fenian threat to New Brunswick, General Doyle visited Saint John to assess the situation for himself. He inspected all the military installations in the city, reviewed separately the Saint John Volunteer Battalion and the British regulars. The regulars in Saint John consisted of only three companies of the 15th Regiment with a strength of 150 men and two artillery batteries of two hundred men. One of the artillery units was a field battery equipped with modern 12-pounder Armstrong guns, but the battery responsible for harbour defence was armed with outdated weapons. To Doyle's chagrin, only ten artillery rounds were available per gun. In addition, an outbreak of Asiatic chol-

A company of the 15th Regiment of Foot (East Yorkshire Regiment), circa 1861. The regiment arrived in New Brunswick in 1861 and served in the province during the Fenian crisis. NBM 14802

era in Saint John threatened the health of the soldiers in the garrison and raised concerns about their accommodation and the sanitation arrangments.

Doyle was quick to take corrective action. Within ten days, the Schooner *Juliet*, towed by HMS *Rosario*, arrived in Saint John loaded with heavy artillery guns, ammunition and four hundred barrels of gunpowder. With the concurrence of the authorities in Britain, the order to rotate the 15th Regiment was rescinded. By the time the 22nd Regiment arrived in Saint John onboard HMS *Simoon* on April 17, arrangements had been made to concentrate the 15th Regiment in Saint John and send the 22nd Regiment to Fredericton. The two companies of the 15th Regiment in Charlottetown were replaced by two companies from Halifax. The 16th Regiment in Halifax, which had been scheduled to rotate to Barbados in early April, was also detained. The 2nd Battalion, 4th Regiment, arrived in Halifax on April 20, followed by the 6th Regiment.

Thanks to Doyle's initiative, by the third week of April, the strength of British regular infantry in New Brunswick and Halifax had doubled.

Concurrent with the increase in British military and naval strength, the provincial militia along the border continued to improve its effectiveness. Based on the intelligence he received, Colonel Anderson strengthened the guards and patrols in St. Andrews, and by mid-April he had sixty men under arms every night. After dark one evening, he loaded the cannon in Market Square with cannister "without exciting much notice," and then he trained two detachments in its use. The St. Andrews *Standard* reported that the Gordon Rifles "were exercised in street protection and fighting, and made quite an imposing appearance, acquitting themselves with credit." To ensure a prompt and effective response, Anderson produced detailed instructions on what action was to be taken when an alert was sounded.

Early in April, Colonels Anderson and Inches consulted on the defence plans for St. Stephen. They agreed that it was not yet necessary to embody the St. Stephen Rifles, but a demanding routine of drills and parades was established. In order to increase the number under arms, additional weapons and ammunition were forwarded from Fredericton. Anderson considered Inches as "probably the most likeable man on the Frontier," and on his recommendation, Gordon appointed Inches commandant of St. Stephen and placed him on full lieutenant colonel's pay. In this capacity, Inches was given wide discretionary powers to act in an emergency. The *Saint Croix Courier* reported on April 14 "Col. Inches has received a telegram from Col. Anderson giving him unlimited powers to act as he sees fit for the defence of this section. This is practical endorsement of the Lieut Colonel's course thus far, and on evidence that his military superiors have every confidence in his judgement and executive capacity."

On the evening of April 8, Anderson sent an urgent message to Colonel Baird to prepare fifty men to send on a moment's notice to St. Andrews. Bugles sounded in the night to assemble the company, creating great excitement among the citizens of Woodstock. By dawn every man in the Woodstock Rifle Company was fully equipped and ready to move. A train on the St. Andrews Railway was detained at the station and prepared to transport the troops. At this inopportune moment, the telegraph lines went down, setting rumours abounding that "St. Andrews had fallen a prey to the invader" and the wires had been deliberately cut to prevent communications with headquarters. When the lines were restored at noon, the volunteers were stood down. However, "scarce had the Rifles assumed their civic attire, when once more the bugle sounded to arms." This time the volunteers remained under arms for twenty-four hours. Being so close to the border, the citizens of Woodstock expressed concern about the safety of their town should the volunteer rifle company be dispatched to defend distant St. Andrews.

Intelligence continued to indicate that a Fenian attack was imminent. The Saint John garrison was placed on high alert, and, after a Fenian schooner was reported moving up the St. Croix River, 120 men were mustered at St. Stephen. At three o'clock in the afternoon of April 10, Gordon ordered Major Simond of the Victoria Rifles in Fredericton to reinforce the St. Andrews garrison with fifty men without delay. An entry in Charles Moffitt's diary for that day reads "Simond came to the shop about 4 p.m. looking for Volunteers to go to St. Andrews to repel an attack of Fenians . . . Tom Fowle & Dal Fowle & Jim Rodger responded to the call." The Fredericton *Headquarters* reported, "There was some little excitement in town . . . when it became known that the Governor had made a call for fifty men, to proceed to St. Andrews. We hear that volunteers from the two City companies — chiefly from Major Simond's Company . . . stepped forth readily." Within four hours the volunteers had assembled in the Masonic Hall where Gordon addressed them. By ten o'clock, the main body under Simond's command was on the road in open wagons, and the next morning thirteen more men followed. The weather was cold and the road was bad. At Dunbarton, the volunteers boarded the train for St. Andrews. Twenty-eight hours after receiving the call, two officers and twenty-eight men arrived in St. Andrews; Ensign Carter's detachment arrived the next day. Assembling this force on such short notice was an amazing feat, considering the distance and the conditions.

Believed to be the York County Militia parading in front of the Court House in Fredericton prior to the departure of Major Edward Simond and the Victoria Rifles for the frontier at St. Andrews on April 9, 1866. PANB P5-151.

Throughout the province there was a spirited call to arms in response to the Fenian threat. The Yeomanry Cavalry of King's County, under command of Captains Otty and Darling, was ready for service and anxiously awaiting the call. On Deer Island, a volunteer rifle company with a strength of fifty-three men formed under the command of Captain James Grew. A volunteer battery of artillery was established in Woodstock. Caught up in the excitement, Alexander "Boss" Gibson, from Marysville just outside Fredericton, offered to raise one hundred men, from the "good strong fellows such as he has constantly in his own employment." His "excellent spirit" received glowing praise in the *Headquarters*.

Although armed men roamed Maine border towns, the presence of the American military was limited. Fort Sullivan had been constructed in 1808 on Clark's Hill, and its cannon dominated the harbour at

Eastport. In 1866, however, its garrison consisted of only sixty-nine men of Company I of the 3rd Artillery Regiment. Sixty-six men of Company M of the same regiment were stationed on Treat's Island off Lubec. The fortifications on Treat's Island had been built during the Civil War as coastal defence against Confederate raiders. To meet the Fenian menace, Company M moved to Eastport on April 27 and was quartered in the French and Sons storehouse. Local newspapers reported that the vacated accommodation on Treat's Island was immediately occupied by frightened refugees from Campobello Island. The only other occupied American military post on the Maine border was Hancock Barracks outside Houlton.

Having received his instructions in Philadelphia from the Secretary of War, General Meade travelled by train to Portland, Maine, where he transferred to the steamer *Regular* for Eastport. Meade brought along sixty-three men from the 1st Heavy Artillery Regiment as reinforcements. Henry J. Murray, the British Consul in Portland, having learned of his schedule, arranged an opportunity to meet with the general as he passed through town. Meade confirmed that his task was to prevent any violation of American neutrality, and he felt confident that he could handle the situation with the military force at his disposal.

Shortly after arriving in Eastport on April 19, Meade ordered the arms and ammunition that had been seized onboard the *Ocean Spray* secured in Fort Sullivan. He estimated that there were three hundred Fenians in town, and he made it clear to their leadership that American neutrality would be enforced in full. Vice Consul Ker had several interviews with Meade during which he outlined British concerns and provided the general with the latest information on the Fenians. Meade telegraphed his headquarters and reported on the *Ocean Spray* seizure. The general then sailed to Calais on the *Regular* for a public meeting in the St. Croix Hall. He thanked the townspeople for their warm reception saying, "he should do his duty here as at Gettysburg." The artillery detachment that Meade had brought with him remained in Calais. General Meade's commanding presence and firm action were reassuring and signalled that peace and order would prevail on the Maine side of the border.

Early April saw a continuous flow of intelligence, all indicating a substantial increase in the number of Fenians along the border and an imminent attack on New Brunswick. The local military and naval commanders agreed that some form of reinforcement by British regulars was required. Colonel Willis in a letter to Gordon wrote "I am decidedly of opinion that a large infantry force and some artillery will be required at St. Andrews or St. Stephen in a very short time." As early as April 10, Gordon had requested that General Doyle forward a company or two to the frontier. Doyle was reluctant to "penny package" his force. He was particularly concerned about desertion by British regulars positioned so close to the American border. On April 14, a very anxious Gordon sent a telegram to Doyle asking, "Does not the emergency justify immediate reinforcement of St. Andrews and St. Stephen with Regulars?" Another telegram followed the next day stating that "war Ships cannot protect St. Stephen" and that British regular soldiers were urgently required on the frontier. Upon receipt of this plea, Doyle acquiesced and responded by saying that he would send not less than a regiment and, if weather permitted, they would embark the next afternoon. Doyle later explained that the force he sent was bigger than Gordon had requested because he felt that "if Troops were sent at all, they must be in such strength, as either to overawe attack, or to repel attack if made, with some degree of certainty." The reinforcements, dubbed the Halifax Field Force, with Doyle in command, embarked on HMS *Duncan* as promised on April 16, arrived the next evening off St. Andrews, and disembarked at Joe's Point on the morning of April 19. The Halifax Field Force consisted of twenty-four officers and 551 men of the 2nd Battalion, 17th Regiment, five officers and sixty-two men of the Royal Artillery, four officers and seventy men of the Royal Engineers and three members of the commissary. As recorded by the *Standard*, the 17th Regiment marched into St. Andrews "preceded by the brilliant band of the 17th, playing soul-stirring strains." As the regiment passed the public square, "the Volunteer Battalion commanded by Major Simond was drawn up in line and presented arms." This impressive show of military might was clearly seen from both sides of the St. Croix River.

Major General George Meade, the senior American military officer on the Maine border during the Fenian crisis. Courtesy of United States National Archives and Records Administration.

Within three weeks, the military situation along the Maine and New Brunswick border had changed dramatically. The provincial militia had established an effective defence line along the border, the Royal Navy dominated Passamaquoddy Bay and the British Army had a substantial field force positioned on the frontier. On the Maine side of the border, Meade was in control, neutrality was being enforced and a large stock of Fenian arms and ammunition had been seized. Killian and his staff faced some hard decisions, but many of their followers had no problem in making a choice. When the steamer *New Brunswick* returned to Portland on April 27, two hundred Fenians were onboard. Murray, the British Consul, reported that after disembarking they headed to the railroad depot and "took almost forcible possession of the train & after a delay of 20 minutes went on to Boston. They were mostly armed with revolvers & fears were entertained of some unpleasant collision occurring on the road. The authorities here were glad to get rid of them in anyway, the police not being powerful enough to control them, & the troops being all away at Eastport." William Grace, one of Killian's lieutenants, on his way home through Portland claimed "the expedition would have been a success had Killian been sustained. He considers O'Mahony an imbecile and a fraud on the public." The recriminations had begun. The Fredericton *Headquarters* summed it up differently: "The Military authorities here and in Halifax, have acted with great promptitude and energy, and have fairly frightened the Fenians from their purpose of invading this province."

St. Croix River with bridge linking St. Stephen N.B. on left with Calais, Maine on right, pre 1894. PANB P364-46

Chapter Nine

The Turning Point

A Boston newspaper article dated April 23, 1866, reported, "The threatened Fenian invasion of the eastern Provinces has bursted and most of those composing the expedition have left Eastport." Nevertheless, on the same day, Vice Consul Ker reported that "Fenian excitement here [Eastport] is still high, alto(*sic*) somewhat abated since last week," and the number of Fenians in town had increased, as they "keep going & coming in squads of 10 or 20." The threat of an invasion may have dissipated, but the Fenians still had the capacity for mischief. A series of incidents occurred in late April and May that kept the border inflamed and the defence forces alert.

The arrival of the Halifax Field Force required a major adjustment by both the local communities and the defence forces. The *Carleton Sentinel* reported "Our sister town St. Andrews is all life and bustle. The red coats of the army and the blue of the navy have created a lively appearance." The editor then coyly noted that, in addition to providing a great sense of security, "the jingle of the silver incident to the sustenance of the army and navy has had, of course, a soothing and salutary effect on the nerves of the system which connect with the purse." It was described as "the gayest summer ever known in St. Andrews with the town full of delightful young officers and ships of war patrolling the St. Croix." With British regulars in St. Andrews, there was no need for the continued presence of the forty-one men of the Victoria Rifles from Fredericton. When they had been despatched, the Fredericton *Headquarters* had expressed the hope that "there will be no need for our Volunteers to show their courage — should there be, we have no doubt about their proving it." Although they saw no action, they acquitted themselves admirably, and the local newspaper reported that "their conduct created a most favourable impression on the minds of the inhabitants," which was reciprocated with hospitality and kindness. Before their departure and in appreciation for their service, the Victoria Rifles were entertained at "an excellent" public dinner held in the St. Andrews Town Hall. Their return trip home on April 27 was much more enjoyable than the one to St. Andrews; Major Simond and his men travelled by railway to Woodstock and then by steamer down the St. John River to Fredericton. On the way through Woodstock, Colonel Baird greeted them with a letter of commendation from Colonel Anderson and the information that they were released from active service. Two days later, Charles Moffitt recorded in his diary that the volunteers in his employ were back to work in his shop.

On Sunday, 22 April, All Saints Anglican Church in St. Andrews held a special service for the garrison, at which the pews were filled to capacity. In addition, all the regular morning services in town were well attended by the military, in particular the Established Church of Scotland. The view of the town's people was expressed in the *St. Andrews Standard,* "It affords us much pleasure to state that the soldiers stationed in this garrison, Regulars and Volunteers, are of the right stuff and that their conduct since their arrival has been unexceptional." In appreciation for the town's hospitality, "the splendid Band of the 17th Regiment" gave concerts in the Court House Square twice weekly, in addition to a special concert held in aid of the building fund for a new church in town.

On April 23, Captain Robert Gibson of HMS *Duncan* hosted local dignitaries from both sides of the border onboard ship. They included the editor of the *Saint Croix Courier*, who wrote a glowing, detailed account of the impressive *Duncan,* its crew and weaponry. He also noted that many of the ship's officers were absent on a fishing expedition, while

Admiral Hope had taken the opportunity for some sightseeing. Hope and his aide had travelled to Woodstock by train and booked into the Blanchard House. The next day, Hope visited the iron works in Upper Woodstock and lunched at the home of the Honourable Charles Connell, returning to St. Andrews on the evening train.

Because St. Stephen was vulnerable to Fenian incursions, consideration was given to reinforcing the town's garrison with British regulars. However, Doyle remained concerned about desertion by troops stationed so close to the American border. When Colonel Anderson implied that reinforcements might not come, Inches wrote to Gordon on April 18 to plead his case, explaining that "the people here have felt much better since they heard there were troops coming . . . & the disappointment should they not come here, will be keenly felt." Immediately after the landing of the Halifax Field Force, Gordon, Doyle and Hope sailed to St. Stephen to assess the situation. After seeing the large number of bridges across the St. Croix River and its narrow width, Doyle informed the Secretary of State for War in London that "nothing would have induced me to put Troops there except the urgent demand of the Lieut Governor and his assurance to me that the Local Force and Inhabitants generally would use every exertion to check desertion." Doyle reluctantly agreed to position 150 regulars in St. Stephen.

Within a week, the agricultural society building had been adapted to accommodate 180 men and four new buildings were erected for a cookhouse, wash room, guardhouse, orderly room and commissary. William Buchanan's stone house was deemed suitable quarters for the officers. On May 3, after several delays, three companies from the 2nd Battalion, 17th Regiment, totalling 150 men, under the command of Major Clement Heigham, sailed up the St. Croix River in HMS *Fawn* and a schooner. Accompanying them were two 6-pounder cannons and one 12-pounder howitzer in the charge of Captain Newman of the Royal Artillery, to be delivered to the recently formed St. Stephen Artillery Battery. Once established in their new quarters on the agricultural grounds, the soldiers were treated to a feast provided by local ladies. More than 250 sat down to dinner, and among the many guests were Colonel Henry and Lieutenant

Wheeler from the United States Army post in Calais. In thanking the citizens of St. Stephen for their warm welcome and the ladies for the wonderful banquet, Doyle displayed his Irish charm saying, "the fair ladies of St. Stephen had done what he hoped the 'Finnegans' never would be permitted to do — take a British General very much by surprise." The detachment of the 17th Regiment stayed in St. Stephen for a week, training and drilling with the local volunteers.

On April 23, an event occurred on the Ferry Point Bridge over the St. Croix River that created an international stir. Privates John Winder and Thomas Hanson of the St. Stephen Rifles were on bridge guard when two men approaching from Calais were identified as Fenians. They were refused entry, and in the heated exchange that followed one of the men said, "we will meet you soon again at the point of the bayonet." While withdrawing, one of the Fenians suddenly drew a pistol and fired at Hanson, but missed. The United States Army guard at the Calais end of the bridge promptly arrested the two Fenians and handed them over to civil authorities. Next day, they were found guilty of drunkenness, fined and released. Under pressure, Governor Samuel Cony of Maine ordered them rearrested. Gordon was considering extradition but a jurisdictional wrangle ensued over the precise point on the bridge from which the shot was fired. Once it was determined that the Fenian had fired from the Maine side of the bridge, jurisdiction fell to Cony. Eventually, the two miscreants were quietly released; however, the incident created sufficient apprehension that USS *De Soto* with 350 American soldiers onboard was despatched to Eastport.

An Eastport resident named Burns had been very helpful to Vice Consul Ker by providing intelligence and assistance. His actions made him very unpopular with the Fenian Brotherhood. One evening, Burns told Ker that he had been threatened and he feared that his property on Indian Island would be destroyed later that night. Knowing firsthand about Fenian terror tactics, Ker contacted Captain Robinson on Campobello in an attempt to obtain protection for Burns' property. The captain of HMS *Pylades,* who was in the area, was also approached. To Ker's great disappointment nothing could be done. On Saturday, April

The Indian Island school house which was fortified as a military outpost during the Fenian crisis. Its strategic position is evident; overlooking Marble Island, Cherry Island to the left and Campobello Island in the distance. PANB P8-300

21, raiders landed on Indian Island and burned four warehouses "to the water's edge." One was a bonded warehouse containing a large consignment of liquor awaiting payment of duties. All the destroyed property, including Burns's, was American owned. In a telegram to the lieutenant-governor, Ker reported the loss as valued at the substantial sum of eight to ten thousand dollars. The Fenians had their revenge.

Although he considered Captain Hood of HMS *Pylades* "a very zealous & diligent officer," Admiral Hope felt "obliged to censure him for not having taken sufficient measures to prevent" the burning of the warehouses. The day after the raid Hope, Doyle and Hood visited Indian Island and concluded that a military post should be established there. After consultation with James Dixon, the customs officer, a recently built but unused school house was selected for a fortified post. Under the direction of a Royal Engineer officer, men from HMS *Rosario* built a palisade around the school, raised an earth embarkment to the window level and sandbagged and loopholed the windows. Initially, one officer and twenty-five sailors formed the garrison until they were replaced by the army. By May 3, Ensign Robert P. Chandler, Sergeant W. Whitlock and nineteen privates from the St. Andrews garrison had relieved the sailors of their post.

A key factor in reducing the tension along the border was the close relationship that existed between Generals Doyle and Meade. For three months, Doyle had been Meade's guest when he commanded the Army of the Potomac during the Civil War. A close friendship based on mutual respect had developed, and they were delighted to find themselves both serving on the Maine border. On April 19, when Meade was in Calais, Doyle paid him a visit, during which they talked at length. Doyle invited Meade to accompany him on his inspection of the St. Stephen Rifles. On May 1, Meade reciprocated by sailing to St. Andrews in the steamer *Regular.* Unfortunately, Meade had developed a bad cold which threatened to become pneumonia and was too ill to leave the ship. The *St. Andrews Standard* reported that the visit onboard "lasted for some time; and on parting, at the insistence of Gen Doyle the band of the 17th Regt, struck up the tune 'Should auld acquaintance be forgot'." Soon after, Meade returned to Philadelphia.

On May 7, Doyle reported that the Fenians were "gradually dispersing." As a result, and with the concurrence of Gordon, he planned to withdraw the Halifax Field Force and replace it with the Saint John Volunteer Battalion in St. Andrews and two companies of the 15th Regiment in St. Stephen. In order to free up accommodation in Halifax, he proposed releasing the 2nd Battalion, 16th Regiment, and permitting it to proceed with its planned rotation to Barbados. After five winters in North America, he was anxious that the battalion reach the West Indies before the hot season, so the soldiers could acclimatize. However, he was adamant that the British forces stationed in New Brunswick should not be reduced because the "local controversy on the subject of Confederation induces the Fenian Leaders to turn their special attention to New Brunswick in the hope of gaining at least sympathy from those most [*sic*] residents opposed to the Plans of Government." Doyle also noted that "the Spirit of the Volunteers, and the zeal with which they have turned out is most praiseworthy, still they need cohesion, and the confidence of support derived from the presence of Regular Troops."

In accordance with Doyle's plan, Colonel Otty received orders on May 8 to prepare his battalion for embarkation to St. Andrews. A similar order was issued to two companies of the 15th Regiment; however, shortly afterward it was rescinded. On May 10, the Saint John Volunteer Battalion marched up Prince William Street from Reed's Point to the Ferry Boat Wharf, led by Otty on horseback and the band of the 15th Regiment. Watched by a crowd estimated at two thousand, the band played "in a masterly manner that appropriate air 'Thou art far away, far away from poor Janette'." The battalion sailed that evening onboard HMS *Simoon*. They disembarked the next morning and occupied the temporary barracks just vacated by the 17th Regiment, while the British regulars occupied the recently emptied berths on HMS *Simoon*. The townspeople of both St. Andrews and St. Stephen regretted seeing the departure of the Halifax Field Force, and as the *St. Andrews Standard* recorded, "during the very brief sojourn of the troops here, they won the respect and good will of the people, which is not surprising; as their good conduct, and kindly feelings would make them favorites anywhere."

Doyle's anxiety concerning desertion by British regular soldiers was well founded. A James Burns was caught trying to assist two privates from the 17th Regiment to desert. He was sentenced to twelve months hard labour in the penitentiary, and the soldiers were returned to their regiment for trial. Privates Carroll and Donnelly of the 17th Regiment absconded from the St. Andrews garrison and after a week on the run they were apprehended by volunteers as they attempted to cross the Porter's Mill Bridge at St. Stephen. When the 17th Regiment returned to Halifax, three of their deserters remained at large. When two soldiers of the 22nd Regiment deserted from the Fredericton garrison, one was captured sixty miles from the city, while the other made his escape. The captured deserter was sentenced to "fifty lashes and be transported for two years."

With so many armed troops along the frontier, mishaps and misfortunes were not unknown. As part of their training the volunteer batteries in Saint John conducted a number of live-fire exercises with their cannon. As noted in the *Morning News*, not all were successful: "During the recent practice by the Volunteers at Dorchester Battery, the windows of the guard room were completely shattered and the building itself was much damaged." Volunteers conducting rifle practice along the banks of St. Croix River had a ball ricochet off the water and nearly strike someone on the Calais side. As the *Saint Croix Courier* glibly remarked, "too great care cannot be exercised in the use of the rifle." Two weeks after arriving in St. Andrews a private in Captain McShane's company of the Saint John Volunteers died of natural causes and was buried with military honours. A sailor who broke his thigh bone falling from a mast on HMS *Cordelia* was reported "in a dangerous state." Another sailor from the *Cordelia* suffered a bizarre accident. While visiting the Turnbull Sash Factory, he was watching with fascination the workings of the planer when suddenly "as if impelled to it in some way, he thrust his hand before the blade, and, in an instant, a portion of it was cut off." Finally, the zeal displayed by the junior officers of HMS *Fawn* when their superiors were absent ashore caused international embarrassment. When they spotted a small boat heading for the Maine shore, they assumed it contained British deserters and fired across its bow. Unfortunately, it was an American pleasure craft containing young women and boys who did not understand the significance of the warning shot and promptly sped up. A second shot was fired directly at the boat. Following the good news and bad news scenario, the good news was that they missed, but the bad news was that the 10-pound shot fetched up a few feet from the door of a clergyman in Robbinston. Word was immediately sent to Eastport and USS *De Soto* was despatched to demand an explanation.

Continued Fenian activity along the St. Croix River kept Colonel Inches and his men alert and wary. On Sunday, May 20, a twelve-oared boat left Eastport for Calais. Inches maintained careful watch on the crew, passengers and cargo, noting that the gathering point was the home of Doyle, the leader of the Calais Fenians. When some of the passengers toured St. Stephen and its neighbourhood, their movements were closely surveilled. Noticing a stranger with a military bearing observing the St.

Stephen Rifles at drill, Inches attempted to engage him in conversation, but when someone referred to Inches as "colonel," the stranger beat a hasty retreat back across the border. When next day a second boat tied up to the first, Inches doubled the guard, made his men sleep with their boots on and he stayed alert all night. After the smaller boat mysteriously left and then returned, Inches and Captain Hutton rowed furtively over to personally check on it. A soldier from Captain Smith's company, on his own initiative, spent a night hidden in a log pile on a Calais wharf, watching and listening, while Doyle and his men loaded a boat only feet from where he lay. These inexplicable Fenian activities maintained the tension along the border.

Ensign Chandler's detachment on Indian Island was relieved by Lieutenant John B. Wilmot and seventeen men of the Saint John Volunteer Battalion. When Wilmot learned that the Fenians were threatening to raid the island again, he took the precaution of increasing the number of sentries from four to six. At last light on May 21, a sentry observed a boat pass Dog Island above Eastport and make its way to Cherry Island where it was joined by a second boat. About midnight, two boats with an estimated ten men in each, using muffled oars, made their way to Marble Island at the end of Indian Island. When challenged by the sentry, a shot was fired from one of the boats. The sentry returned fire and an exchange of shots quickly followed. Using a rocket, Lieutenant Wilmot immediately signalled HMS *Niger,* which was stationed off Campobello. Within twenty-five minutes, *Niger* responded with two boatloads of marines. With the volunteers on neighbouring Campobello also fully alerted, the Fenians fled into the night. The intent of the raiders was never made clear.

At about midnight on Wednesday, May 30, the citizens of St. Andrews were rudely disturbed from their slumbers "by the drums of HMS *Cordelia* beating to quarters, the firing of musketry, and the tramping of men and horses." It was a calm but dark night, and it was not possible to discern the source of the disturbance. "In a few minutes a big gun from the *Cordelia* was discharged, and then another, which was promptly answered by one from the battery at Fort Tipperary, followed by the bugles

"St. Andrews Harbour and Bay, New Brunswick, 1862," showing the town of St Andrews, the harbour, Navy Island and Passamaquoddy Bay from the area of Joe's Point. PANB P4-3-62

at the Barracks sounding the assembly and the alarm, which led to a general rush to arms." The town's people feared the long awaited Fenian attack was underway. The Saint John Volunteers, Gordon Rifles, volunteer battery and home guard assembled immediately in accordance with their training. It was reported "that within five minutes the ammunition wagons were filled, the rifles strapped on, and the guns ready for action." Although some volunteers had not taken the time to fully dress, they stood ready to face the foe. The sound of the heavy guns firing carried down the Bay of Fundy to St. George. It created a similar commotion there as the volunteers of St. George rushed to arms and manned their defences.

Amidst the turmoil, people feared for their lives and the safety of their property. As the volunteers ran off to their battle stations, their families were left to fend for themselves. The wife of Corporal Levi Handy of the

Gordon Rifles, alone and uncertain what to do, was terrified. She bundled up her children and hid them in the garden behind the house, after posting her fifteen year old son at the corner of their house with the family shotgun, instructing him to shoot on sight anyone approaching the yard. Luckily, it was daylight before Corporal Handy returned home.

During the pandemonium, Colonel Anderson displayed the leadership for which he was noted. He immediately dispatched an officer to ascertain the cause of the firing and within half an hour had the answer. It was a naval regulation that once a quarter every British warship was to practise repelling a surprise night assault using blank ammunition. Commander de Wahl of HMS *Cordelia* choose that night, while anchored snugly in the harbour of St. Andrews, to exercise his crew forgetting the tense atmosphere that existed in the town. The naval exercise was a success. It was "a minute and a half from the drums beating the men turned out and firing commenced." Anderson quickly turned the awkward situation to his advantage by declaring it an unscheduled exercise. He was reported as saying "Commander de Wahl deserves the thanks of the people, for testing by his practice the courage of our Volunteers, they were up to the mark, and that in a very few minutes." Everyone returned home extremely pleased with their performances and their displays of loyalty. Unfortunately, no one in St. Andrews was aware that the people of St. George were also on high alert, and it took some time before they got the word.

Throughout May, the Fenians along the border continued to disperse. Funding had run out, and many experienced difficulties paying rent and buying food. The American government offered free railway tickets to assist them on their way. The *Carleton Sentinel* reported on June 1 that "The First Regiment of Massachuset Fenians, numbering about eighty or one hundred men, has returned from the 'Seat of War' dispirited and demoralized. They are very bitter in their denunciations of the leaders; but expect to start again soon under more favorable auspices." The aborted invasion left the O'Mahony faction of Fenian Brotherhood in disarray. Killian was blamed for the failed military venture and expelled from the movement. O'Mahony's treasury had been depleted, and he was forced

Chapter Ten

The Legacy

The memory of the unsuccessful Fenian invasion across the Maine border and the fear it created along the New Brunswick frontier has been all but forgotten. The participants in the crisis are long departed and so too are their stories, both factual and embellished. There is no historic site or marker in New Brunswick to recount these stirring events. However, the legacy of the Fenian crisis left a mark on both the province and Canada.

Lieutenant-Governor Gordon was proud of the performance of the volunteers during the Fenian crisis, a performance that justified the effort that he and his staff had made to revitalize the New Brunswick militia. Gordon's contribution was acknowledged in the Saint John *Morning News*: "We cannot too highly commend the energy displayed by our Commander-in-Chief." Gordon visited the volunteer units to pass on his compliments personally and acknowledge his pleasure publicly in the Militia General Orders:

> His Excellency desires to express the gratification he has experienced in finding the officers, noncommissioned officers and men composing the Force engaged in protecting those points of the Frontier most threatened by attack, deserving of his entire confidence. His Excellency is fully aware that upon them developed duties of a particular difficult nature,

the discharge of which was occasionally attended with a greater degree of hardship than His Excellency had anticipated or desired, but which have been accomplished to His Excellency's full satisfaction.

In addressing the opening of the June 1866 session of the legislative assembly, Gordon acknowledged the support received from Britain, "You will, I doubt not, concur with me in the expression of gratitude for the promptitude with which the aid of Her Majesty's Navy and military force was rendered on that occasion, and the magnitude of the scale on which it was afforded." Gordon soon learned that he had been promoted to the governorship of Trinidad; he sailed from Saint John on October 1, 1866, to assume his new appointment in the British West Indies.

The Fenian crisis posed an external threat, which gave the people of New Brunswick a common and shared military experience, enhancing their sense of community and loyalty. In particular, it heightened public interest in defence matters and the volunteer movement flourished across the province. The Camp of Instruction held in July 1866 at Camp Torryburn, outside Saint John, was another major success. The camp emphasized training officers and officer aspirants in order to address the shortage of trained militia officers experienced during the Fenian crisis. It became a fixed feature of Canadian defence policy that the militia would be based on a small but active volunteer force. This concept, which saw Canada through two world wars, is the military legacy inherited from Lieutenant-Governor Gordon and the Fenian crisis.

The memory of the Fenians waxed and waned. Thirty years later, in January 1899, Joseph Chamberlain, the British Colonial Secretary, announced that "Her Majesty the Queen has been graciously pleased to approve" a commemorative medal for the Fenian Raids and the Red River Expedition of 1870. This decision sparked renewed public interest in the Canadian military and pride in the loyalty and dedication shown by its volunteers. Since the medal was issued only to survivors, identifying and locating those entitled to "the coveted trophy" presented a problem; the search engendered considerable public and media interest. In time,

The Canada General Service Medal with Fenian 1866 bar was awarded to Private James Von Buren Spinney of Captain James Bogue's Company, 2nd Battalion Charlotte County Militia. Courtesy of the George Branch of the Royal Canadian Legion.

ceremonial parades were held at which the medals were presented, amid a wave of patriotism that was sweeping the country as a result of the South African War. Twelve years later, and forty-six years after the departure of the Fenians, the crisis again became front page news. The federal government offered surviving veterans of the Fenian Raids or their widows a one hundred dollar cash bonus. The *Fenian Raid Volunteer Bounty Act*, proclaimed in April 1912, provided the bounty for anyone enlisted in the militia and called out in 1866, and an amendment provided the bounty to the widows of qualified deceased veterans. It was widely considered a crass ploy by Sir Robert Borden's Conservative government: using public money to gain votes. Be that as it may, it kept the memory of the Fenian crisis and the role played by the volunteers alive in the public's mind.

However, it was the political impact of the Fenian crisis that left the most enduring legacy. The debate over Confederation had been raging in British North America for a number of years when, on January 30, 1865, the premier of New Brunswick, the Honourable Samuel Leonard Tilley, dissolved the legislative assembly. A hotly contested election followed over the question of whether New Brunswick should join Confederation. Tilley and his pro-Confederation party were humiliated and suffered a major defeat. On March 6, Tilley resigned and handed the government over to Albert James Smith, who left no doubt that his goal was to keep New Brunswick out of Confederation. Nor did Lieutenant-Governor Gordon support Confederation, favouring instead a union of the Atlantic provinces.

The whole concept of a British North American union was in serious jeopardy, but times and men change. The British government made it clear that it, and Queen Victoria herself, considered Confederation desirable, and overnight Gordon became a strong advocate. Pressure from Gordon and the inability of the anti-Confederates to form a cohesive party to tackle such pressing problems as reciprocity, railway policy and the Fenians rendered the Smith government unsustainable. On May 9, 1866, it resigned and Gordon dissolved the provincial parliament. With the Fenian crisis as a backdrop, the opposing parties fought an election during May and June. Tilly and the pro-Confederates campaigned on the issues of loyalty to the British Crown, the blessings of the British connection and the dangers of American republicanism. Hanging over all was the Fenian crisis and the defence question. All of the discussion over the past five years concerning imperial defence had acquired pertinence. The *St. Croix Courier* summarized the situation:

> If there is one argument in favor of Union stronger than another, it is the necessity that exists for a good and efficient system of mutual defense. We have sometimes regarded this as one of the weaker points in favor of Union, invasion or trouble seemed to be at so great a distance, but now when we see how soon sudden danger can threaten us, and how our enemies may concentrate within a gunshot of our doors, the man must be blind, infatuated or prejudiced who can fail to recognize its force.

For the pro-Confederates, the Fenian crisis was a blessing. Tilley and his party won a sweeping victory, taking all counties except Gloucester, Kent and Westmorland, areas where the Fenian scare had appeared remote. He won sixty percent of the vote and thirty-three seats to Smith's eight. Thanks to the intervention of the Fenians, New Brunswick was firmly set on the path to Confederation. Without New Brunswick, there would have been no Confederation, and without Confederation there could be no modern Canada. Canada is the real legacy of the Fenian crisis of 1866.

Glossary of Terms

Armstrong Gun – The Armstrong gun was a wrought-iron breech-loading rifled cannon manufactured by Sir William Armstrong & Co in England. It was adopted for service in the British navy and army in 1859. In its day, it was considered the leading edge of technology, revolutionizing the use of artillery.

Artillery – Artillery is the branch of the army that employs cannons.

Battalion – A battalion is a unit of infantry consisting of a number of companies, normally with an establishment of five hundred men.

Battery – A battery is a unit or sub-unit of artillery consisting of four to six guns.

British North America – British North America was the term used after the American Revolution and prior to Confederation, referring to all of the British colonies and territories existing in North America.

British regular – A British regular was a professional full-time soldier, libel for service anywhere in the British Empire.

Called-out – Being called-out is a colloquial term for being embodied. See embodied below.

Canada – The Act of Union of 1841 reunified Upper Canada and Lower Canada under one government, establishing the Province of Canada. In 1866, the term Canada referred to what is today the provinces of Quebec and Ontario.

Cannister – Cannister is a projectile fired from a cannon consisting of a tin container filled with lead balls.

Cavalry – Cavalry is a unit of horse-mounted soldiers. In 1866, cavalry was normally employed in reconnaissance and as despatch riders.

Coehorn – A very short cannon or mortar, the coehorn, which was named after its designer, was used for high or curved trajectory firing.

Commander-in-Chief – The commander-in-chief is the person responsible for all of the military land forces in a given region. In 1866, Lieutenant-Governor Gordon was the commander-in-chief in New Brunswick.

Company – A company is a sub-unit of an infantry battalion, with a normal establishment of fifty men.

Embody – When a militiaman is embodied, he is formally ordered by the government to perform active military service. During the period of being embodied the militiaman is paid.

HMS – Her Majesty's Ship, referring to a ship of the British Royal Navy.

Howitzer – A howitzer is a short-barrelled cannon designed for high-angle fire.

Infantry – Infantry are foot soldiers. In 1866, they were normally armed with rifles and bayonets.

Lower Provinces – The lower provinces were those colonies in British North America that bordered on the Atlantic Ocean, with the exception of Quebec.

Marine – A marine is a soldier who serves on board a ship or who works closely with naval forces.

Spencer Rifle – When the 7-shot repeating Spencer Rifle was brought into action in August 1863 during the American Civil War, it was the most advanced infantry weapon on the battlefield. The British Army had nothing equivalent to it, and to have Fenians armed with the Spencer would have posed a major concern.

Subaltern – A subaltern is a junior commissioned officer holding the rank of ensign, lieutenant or captain.

USS – United States Ship, referring to a ship of the United States Navy.

Zouaves – Zouaves were originally French light infantry from Algeria. Their unique "Oriental" uniforms appealed to some volunteers.

Key Personalities in the Fenian Crisis

Anderson, Thomas, Lieutenant Colonel – Anderson, previously the adjutant general of the New Brunswick Militia, commanded the Frontier District headquartered in St. Andrews.

Archibald, Edward – Archibald was the British consul general in New York City.

Baird, William Teed, Lieutenant Colonel – Baird was the commanding officer of the 1st Battalion Carleton County Militia and deputy quartermaster general of the New Brunswick Militia.

Boggs, Acting Rear Admiral – Boggs commanded the United States Navy's Eastern Squadron.

Bogue, James, Captain – Bogue was the commanding officer of a Class A infantry company equipped with cannon in St. George.

Bolton, James, Captain – Bolton was the commanding officer of a Class A infantry company in St. George.

Boyd, James, Lieutenant Colonel – Boyd was temporarily replaced as commanding officer of the 1st Battalion Charlotte County Militia and a member of legislative assembly for St. Andrews.

Brown, James, Lieutenant Colonel – Brown commanded the 3rd Battalion Charlotte County Militia headquartered on Deer Island.

Bruce, Sir Frederick – Bruce was the British ambassador in Washington.

Bryon, Luke, Captain – Bryon was the officer commanding the Class A infantry company on Campobello.

Cole, John Amber, Brevet Colonel – Cole was the colonel of the 15th Regiment and commander of British troops and militia on active service in New Brunswick.

Crookshank, Robert W., Lieutenant Colonel – Crookshank replaced Robertson as commanding officer of the Saint John Volunteer Battalion.

Dixon, James – Dixon was the New Brunswick customs officer on Indian Island in Passamaquoddy Bay.

Doyle, Sir Charles Hastings, Major General – Doyle commanded the British Forces in the lower provinces.

Doyle, Dennis – Doyle was the leader of the Fenian circle in Calais, Maine.

Foster, Stephen K., Lieutenant Colonel – Foster commanded the New Brunswick Regiment of Artillery.

Gordon, Arthur Hamilton, first Lord Stanmore – Gordon was appointed lieutenant-governor of New Brunswick and commander-in-chief in October 1861.

Grierson, Lieutenant Colonel – Grierson was the lieutenant colonel commanding the British 15th Regiment.

Hallowes, H. J., Captain – Hallowes of the British 15th Regiment was aide-de-camp to Gordon and commander of the 1865 Camp of Instruction.

Hood, Arthur W. A., Captain – Hood was captain of HMS *Pylades*.

Hope, Sir James, Vice Admiral – Hope commanded the British North American and West Indies Squadron.

Inches, James Archibald, Lieutenant Colonel – Inches was the commanding officer of the 4th Battalion Charlotte County Militia and commandant of the St. Stephen garrison.

James, Robert D., Major – Jones was the commanding officer of the St. Andrews Home Guard.

Ker, Robert – Ker was the British vice consul in Eastport, Maine.

Killian, Bernard Doran – Killian was the secretary treasurer of the Fenian Brotherhood, an O'Mahony supporter, and senior Fenian military leader on the Maine border.

Long, Washington – Long was the United States collector of customs in Eastport, Maine.

Maunsell, George Joseph, Lieutenant Colonel – Maunsell was adjutant general of the New Brunswick Militia.

Meade, George, Major General – A famous veteran of the Civil War, Meade was senior American military officer on the Maine border.

Murray, Henry J. – Murray was British consul in Portland, Maine.

O'Mahony, John – O'Mahony founded the Fenian Brotherhood in North America.

Osborne, Henry, Captain – Osborne was the officer commanding the artillery battery in St. Andrews.

Otty, Andrew, Lieutenant Colonel – Otty was the deputy adjutant general of the New Brunswick Militia and commanding officer of the Saint John Volunteer Battalion replacing Crookshank.

Pheasant, Edward, Captain – Pheasant commanded the St. Andrews Class A Gordon Rifles.

Pick, George H., Captain – Pick was the officer commanding one of the Saint John volunteer artillery batteries.

Roberts, William Randall – Roberts was elected president of the Fenian Brotherhood senate in October 1865 and was leader of the Roberts faction.

Robertson, John, the Honourable, Lieutenant Colonel – A member of the legislative assembly, Robertson was the commanding officer of the Saint John Volunteer Battalion. He resigned in December, 1865.

Robinson, Captain – Robinson was the senior militia officer on Campobello Island.

Rose, William T., Captain – Rose was the officer commanding the St. Stephen artillery battery.

Seward, William H. – Seward was the secretary of state in the United States government.

Simond, Edward, Major – Simond commanded the Victoria Rifles of Fredericton, a Class A infantry company.

Smith, Albert James, the Honourable – Smith was premier of New Brunswick from March 6, 1865, to May 9, 1866, and leader of the anti-Confederate party.

Stephen, James – Stephen was leader of the Irish Republican Brotherhood in Ireland.

Strickland, George, Captain – Strictland was the officer commanding the Class A Woodstock Rifle Company.

Sweeny, Thomas, Brigadier General – A distinguished veteran of the Union Army, Sweeny was elected secretary of war of the Fenian Brotherhood and the military leader of the Roberts faction.

Thurgar, John, Lieutenant Colonel – Thurgar was the commanding officer of the Saint John City Rifles.

Tilley, Samuel Leonard, the Honourable – Tilley was premier of New Brunswick between 1861-65 and 1866-67, and leader of the pro-Confederate party.

Tupper, James Rice, Lieutenant Colonel – Tupper commanded the 2nd Battalion Carleton County Militia in Florenceville.

Wetmore, Douglas, Lieutenant Colonel – Wetmore was the commanding officer of the 2nd Battalion Charlotte County Militia in St. George.

Williams, William Fenwick, Major General – Williams was the general officer commanding British regular forces in Canada.

Willis, Cuthbert, Major – Willis was the acting commanding officer of the 1st Battalion Charlotte County Militia and commandant of the St. Andrews garrison.

Wilmot, Lemuel the Honourable, Lieutenant Colonel – Wilmot was the commanding officer of the 1st Battalion York County Militia and a member of the legislative assembly.

Wilson, D., Major – Wilson, a member of the York County Militia, was temporary second-in-command of the Saint John Volunteer Battalion.

Photo Credits

Photos and other illustrative material on the cover; on pages 10, 18, 20, 30, 38, 58, 61, 68, 69, 81, 89, 94, 99, and 104 appear courtesy of the Provincial Archives of New Brunswick (PANB); and on pages 8, 45, 54, 70, 75, and 86 courtesy of the New Brunswick Museum (NBM); on page 41 courtesy of Valerie Teed; on page 48 courtesy of Harold Wright; on page 56 courtesy of Archives and Special Collections, Harriet Irving Archives, University of New Brunswick; on page 66 courtesy of the Charlotte County Archives; on page 77 courtesy of the United States Naval Historical Center, New Hampshire; on page 82 courtesy of the National Library of Australia; on page 85 courtesy of the Maritime Museum of the Atlantic; on page 92 courtesy of the United States National Archives and Records Administration; and on the back cover courtesy of the St. George Branch of the Royal Canadian Legion. The maps on pages 12, 27, and 42 are by Mike Bechthold. All illustrative material is reproduced by permission.

Selected Bibliography

Primary Sources

St. Andrews Garrison Orders Book from 26 March 1866 to 15 June 1866. Privately owned.

Regimental Letter Book #17, New Brunswick Regiment of Artillery.

Letter Book of Captain, later Major, Darell R. Jago, assistant adjutant general of artillery. Property of Heritage Resources, Saint John.

"Journal of Carleton County Home Guard for period December 1865 to December 1866 by Lieutenant-Colonel W. T. V Baird." Transcription by R. Wallace Hale. Held in Raymond Collection of the L.P. Fisher Public Library in Woodstock, NB.

Printed Sources

Baird, W. T. *Seventy Years of New Brunswick Life*. Saint John: George E. Day, 1890.

Cameron, James M. *Fenian Times in Nova Scotia*. Collections of the Nova Scotia Historical Society. Kentville, NS: Kentville Publishing Co. Ltd., 1970.

Chapman, J.K. *The Career of Arthur Hamilton Gordon, First Lord Stanmore 1829-1912*. Toronto: University of Toronto Press, 1964.

D'Arcy, William. *The Fenian Movement in the United States 1858-1886: A Dissertation*. Washington: Catholic University of America Press, 1947.

Davis, Harold A. "The Fenian Raid on New Brunswick."*Canadian Historical Review*. Volume XXXVI, No. 4 (December 1955), 316-334.

Facey-Crowther, David R. *The New Brunswick Militia 1787-1867*. Fredericton: New Brunswick Historical Society, 1990.

MacDonald, John A., Captain. *Troublous Times in Canada: A History of the Fenian Raids of 1866 and 1870*. Toronto: W. S. Johnson, 1910.

McDonald, R. H. *A Narrative and Structural History of Carleton Martello Tower.* Manuscript Report Number 233. National Historic Parks and Sites Branch, Parks Canada, 1978.

MacNutt, W. S. *New Brunswick: A History, 1784-1867*. Toronto: Macmillan, 1963.

Maunsell, George J. Lieutenant-Colonel. "The New Brunswick Militia." *The New Brunswick Magazine*. Volume II, Number 3 (January-June 1899), 123-132.

Marquis, Greg. *In Armageddon's Shadow: The Civil War and Canada's Maritime Provinces.* Montreal and Kingston: McGill-Queen's University Press, 1998.

Neidhardt, W. S. *Fenianism in North America.* University Park, PA and London: Pennsylvania State University Press, 1975.

Senior, Hereward. *The Last Invasion of Canada: The Fenian Raids 1866-1870.* Toronto and Oxford: Dundurn Press, 1991.

Sturdee, Major E. T. *Historical Records of the 62nd St. John Fusiliers (Canadian Militia).* Saint John, NB: J. & A. McMillan, 1888.

Thyen, John R. (ed.). *Canada General Service Medal Roll 1866-70.* Winnipeg, MB: Bunker To Bunker Books, 1998.

Vesey, Maxwell. "When New Brunswick Suffered Invasion." *The Dalhousie Review*. (5 January 1940), 197-204.

Wilson, J. Brent. "That Vast Experiment: The New Brunswick Militia's 1865 Camp of Instruction." *Canadian Military History*. Volume 6, Number 2 (Autumn 1997), 39-53.

Acknowledgements

I wish to thank the many people who assisted me in bringing this volume to print. Special thanks go to Sheila Washburn who approached me with documents that she had inherited from her father Earl Caughey's estate. They immediately sparked considerable excitement as they proved to be original documents pertaining to the Fenian crisis in St. Andrews. With Sheila's approval, they became the genesis of this book. Research was facilitated by the cheerful response I always received to my many requests from Janice Cook, archivist, Provincial Archives of New Brunswick, and I benefitted from her ability to track down obscure documents and images. In addition, the staff of the Charlotte County Archives was only too willing to drop what they were doing to assist, in particular archivist Charlotte McAdam and volunteer Janet Craig. As always, Harold E. Wright of Heritage Resources in Saint John was ready to share his extensive knowledge and resources of New Brunswick history. Without hesitation, R. Wallace Hale of the Carleton County Historical Society provided his useful transcription of Lieutenant Colonel Baird's Journal. Valerie Teed's spontaneous response to a request from a total stranger for assistance was more than could be expected. Many thanks go to my friend of long standing, Colonel Roger Acreman, who patiently endured repeated tales of Fenians and still found time to critique the draft manuscript. Without the faith displayed in me by Marc Milner and Brent Wilson, the directors of the New Brunswick Military Heritage Project, nothing would have been possible, and in particular the guidance and assistance provided by Brent is greatly appreciated. Finally, it was my wife Sharon who, at the critical times, provided essential encouragement and kept me focused.

Index

The New Brunswick Military Heritage Project

The New Brunswick Military Heritage Project, a non-profit organization devoted to public awareness of the remarkable military heritage of the province, is an initiative of the Brigadier Milton F. Gregg, VC, Centre for the Study of War and Society of the University of New Brunswick. The organization consists of museum professionals, teachers, university professors, graduate students, active and retired members of the Canadian Forces, and other historians. We welcome public involvement. People who have ideas for books or information for our database can contact us through our Web site: www.unb.ca/nbmhp.

One of the main activities of the New Brunswick Military Heritage Project is the publication of the New Brunswick Military Heritage Series with Goose Lane Editions. This series of books is under the direction of Marc Milner, Director of the Gregg Centre, and J. Brent Wilson, Research Director of the Gregg Centre at the University of New Brunswick. Publication of the series is supported by a grant from the Canadian War Musuem.

Canadian
War Museum

Musée canadien
de la guerre

The New Brunswick Military Heritage Project

Volume 1
Saint John Fortifications, 1630-1956, Roger Sarty and Doug Knight

Volume 2
Hope Restored: The American Revolution and the Founding of New Brunswick, Robert L. Dallison

Volume 3
The Siege of Fort Beauséjour, 1755, Chris M. Hand

Volume 4
Riding into War: The Memoir of a Horse Transport Driver, 1916-1919, James Robert Johnston

Volume 5
The Road to Canada: The Grand Communications Route from Saint John to Quebec, W. E. (Gary) Campbell

Volume 6
Trimming Yankee Sails: Pirates and Privateers of New Brunswick, Faye Kert

Volume 7
War on the Home Front: The Farm Diaries of Daniel MacMillan, 1914-1927, ed. Bill Parenteau and Stephen Dutcher

About the Author

Robert Leonard Dallison attended both the Royal Roads Military College and the Royal Military College of Canada, and following graduation in 1958, was commissioned into the Princess Patricia's Canadian Light Infantry. He received a B.A. (History) from R.M.C. and a B.A. (History & International Studies) from the University of British Columbia. He served for thirty-five years with the Canadian Army, obtaining the rank of lieutenant colonel, and ending his career as Chief of Staff of the Combat Arms School at CFB Gagetown. After retiring, he maintained his life long interest in history and heritage, including serving as the President of Fredericton Heritage Trust and the New Brunswick representative on the Board of Governors for Heritage Canada. From 1992 to 2002, he was Director of Kings Landing Historical Settlement. Retired again, he is currently living with his wife Sharon in Fredericton. He is author of *Hope Restored: The American Revolution and the Founding of New Brunswick* (2003), volume 2 of the NBMHP's book series.